THE RHYTHM OF LIFE

David Adam is the Vicar of Holy Island where his work involves ministering to thousands of pilgrims and other visitors. He was born in Alnwick, Northumberland, and worked as a coal miner before being ordained. During more than twenty years as Vicar of Danby in North Yorkshire he discovered a gift for composing prayers in the Celtic pattern. Since 1985 he has published several very popular collections of prayers and meditations based on the Celtic tradition, using material he has tried and tested with groups and individuals from his own parishes and on retreat.

Also by David Adam

The Edge of Glory: Prayers in the Celtic Tradition
(Morehouse 1987)

The Cry of the Deer: Meditations on the Hymn of St. Patrick
(Morehouse 1988)

The Open Gate: Celtic Prayers for Growing Spiritually
(Morehouse 1995)

THE RHYTHM OF LIFE

Celtic Daily Prayer

———

DAVID ADAM

———

Illustrations by
Jean Freer

MOREHOUSE PUBLISHING

First published 1996
SPCK

Copyright © David Adam 1996

First U.S. edition published in 1997 by:

Morehouse Publishing
P.O. Box 1321
Harrisburg, PA 17105

*A catalog record of this book is available from the
Library of Congress.*

Printed in the United States of America

To my mother, Mary
who found great strength from the Psalms
in her last illness.

Contents

——

Introduction

The rhythm of life on the island of Lindisfarne where I live is ordered not only by the tides and the seasons but by the daily ringing of the church bell for prayer. People are made aware of the fact that prayer is being said early in the morning and again in the evening. Many of the visitors to the island come and share in the daily prayers. Every day we say Morning and Evening Prayer and celebrate the Eucharist, and several people have expressed a wish that they could continue this pattern in some way when they return to their homes. They would like to establish fixed times for prayer which will enrich the whole day and guide them through it, while also keeping a link with the whole wide church at prayer. Some have asked for a pattern of prayer for the week. Out of this has arisen this series of 'little offices' to help people to rejoice constantly in the presence of the living God.

The use of the word 'office' dates back to the beginnings of the monastic movement in the early centuries of the church, and was originally used to acknowledge the *officium*, or duty, of each Christian to pray daily with the whole church. The daily office was meant to meet the need for more public prayers and psalms than were found in the Communion service, prayers which could be said by people at home, as well as by the monks in church. Because most people could not read, and in any case books were not available, the office by its nature needed to be short, and something that could easily be committed to memory. It was intended to be part of the public daily prayers of the church, and to build up shared worship in the community.

The acts of worship in this book are designed to

be complete in themselves, and simple to use. The Bible readings are purposely short so that they can be memorized. Likewise, the prayers are written in such a way that they can soon be learned off by heart, simply by regular recitation. I am a great believer in 'recital theology' – that is, to get the word off the page and into the mind and the heart. For this reason it is good whenever possible to say the prayers aloud. By reciting aloud, we use our eyes, mouth and ears as well as our minds. Reading aloud produces a physical vibration that affects not only our ears but our heart and our mind also, so that when we hear the words in a different context an echoing chord is struck in our being, setting off a whole melody of associations. Once we have words in our heart, a phrase, or even a single word, can pluck at our heartstrings and cause us to react.

When we celebrate in worship the mighty acts of God, we are not so much concerned with re-membering as with entering into the events; we are emphasising the eternal rather than the historical. We need to be open to the fact that what we are celebrating, because it is eternal, is here and now. It is *now* that our Lord comes, it is *now* that he is born among us, it is *now* that he is seen among us, it is *now* that the risen Lord appears. In the same way it is *now* that the Father is creating and re-creating. It is *now* that the Spirit descends. Our celebrations tune us in to the eternal events, allow us to respond to them and to carry that response into our daily living. Thus the rhythm of prayer resonates throughout the day.

We are not just reading or acting out the great events of God, we are partaking in them. We celebrate Advent with the assurance that our Lord comes, and comes to us here and now. In the same manner we seek to meet the incarnate Lord who dwells among us. The betrayal, rejection, crucifixion and death of our Lord weave their way through our streets, our homes and our lives. We need to be sensitive to the redeeming love and salvation that is now at work in us, as we also need to be aware of the many deaths and resurrections that are experienced by us. I believe in the resurrection of the body for it is an on-going fact. The whole of the liturgical year is a mystery, joyful, sorrowful and glorious, that is at work in us and through us. We need to become more aware of these rhythms in our life.

Each 'little office' should have some link with Sunday worship, so that the one enriches the other. One of the great weaknesses of the church today is that people have stopped praying in their homes; or if they do pray, their prayer often has no link with the church or liturgy and so does not resonate with them. Without daily Bible reading and ordered prayer, it is hard for our Sunday worship to strike a chord. But if through daily prayer and a build-up of images the Sunday worship plucks at certain strings, then all are enriched. Once we have built up a collection of phrases and sayings which we have meditated on, every time they are used they echo and re-echo in the depths of our lives. When we have the office by heart we can use it at any spare minute in the day until it truly vibrates in our life – better, until He truly vibrates in our life.

Once, when caring for an elderly lady who was dying, I was made aware of the great wealth we can carry in our hearts and minds. Very near to death, she said to me, 'Let us say a few psalms.' In fact, she said them and I listened. As the great themes rolled out from that frail body I knew what strength they contained. 'I will lift up my eyes to the hills . . . my help comes from the Lord', 'The Lord is my shepherd . . . Though I walk through the valley of the shadow of death I will fear no evil.' Each phrase or psalm seemed to suggest another. She passed away in peace whilst revealing the wealth she had obtained from the scriptures and psalms. Mere words had become the vehicle for the living Word of God. This was no theory or sedative, but a vital relationship with a living Lord. So this is the reasoning behind having a short psalm with a response and a short scripture reading with a response. Soon the responses, at least, will become part of our daily routine — and then the whole ethos of the readings will pervade our lives. The written word will become a gate for the living Word to enter our midst.

The idea of having four daily offices or services is not just a convenient way to mark morning, noon, evening and night, but to give variety to the theme for the day and to allow people to choose freely between one or another of the daily offices. A person who wants, or has time for, only one office a day will have enough for twenty-eight days. But I also feel it is good to use the same office every day for a while, until it is truly absorbed into the heart and mind. The obvious way to do that is to use the Advent Office (Saturday Night) in the Advent season, the Christmas Office (Tuesday) in the Christmas season, and so on.

Wherever possible these are prayers to be shared, as family prayers or in small groups. They can suitably be used at the beginning of a meeting, or at the beginning of an informal church service. The whole aim is to be flexible, and to let the prayers resonate and reveal the rhythm of life.

THE STRUCTURE OF THE SERVICES
The layout for all the services is basically the same; only the midday office differs slightly. The aim is to give a meditative and structured pattern to our daily prayers.

The pattern is to strengthen our church worship and to be strengthened by it. But above all it is a gateway to the eternal realities and to an awareness of the presence of our God. The basic components of the acts of worship are as follows:

Affirmation
Silence
Acclamations and responses
Psalm
'Little Chapter' (scripture reading)
Canticle (omitted at the Midday Office)
Kyries (see page 123. These are extended at the Midday Office)
The Lord's Prayer
Intercessions (At the Midday Office these are combined with the Kyries)
Collect or prayer
Affirmation
The Grace, or a Blessing Prayer.

The Affirmation is to place in the heart and the mind the theme for the day – to affirm what we say we believe. This helps us to realise that all of God's actions are taking place in our lives and in our world. The affirmation at the end of the service is about God's relationship to us. We are not requesting this relationship; it is a fact and we are seeking to be aware of it. It is good to repeat these affirmations throughout the day between services, until they become part of our awareness of our God. Their function is to open our senses and our lives to the reality that is about us.

Silence is important. It is to be a time of eager waiting upon and watching for our God, a time to let the affirmations go deep into our way of thinking and acting. It is not an empty time but a God-filled time, when we open ourselves up to him. It is good to decide beforehand how long the silence will be.

Acclamations and Responses. These are linked to the theme for the day. Once again the purpose is to get us deeper into the realities of our faith, to open ourselves to the mighty works of God. The responses are in bold print, and it is hoped that groups will respond vigorously.

The Psalms from the Old Testament have enriched Jewish and Christian worship for centuries. If the group has only one book, the psalm can be said by the leader and the refrain, printed in bold print, repeated by everyone after each verse. Alternatively, the verses can be said alternately by the leader and the group, or by two groups alternately. Or the refrain can be said at the beginning and end only. I like to say the refrain quietly between each verse, especially as it is linked to the theme for the day. After each psalm the Gloria may be added (see page 123).

The 'Little Chapter' is always a quotation from the scriptures. (I have used the New Revised Standard Version.) It is a way of using the scriptures as developed in monastic services, so that the people, who had no Bible of their own, could memorise them and carry them in their heart. Here it is used so that you may soon not only have read it but learned it off by heart and inwardly digested its message. It is purposely short so that it is easy to carry around in the heart and mind.

The Canticles are acts of prayer and praise taken mainly from the scriptures. The canticles used here come from the *Alternative Service Book* of the Church of England unless stated otherwise. When a canticle is indicated as being based on a passage of scripture, it is taken directly from the New Revised Standard

Version, Anglicized Edition. The refrain can be used as suggested for the Psalms, and the Gloria can also be added.

After the canticle can follow the creed and/or the confession (see page 124). It is good to include them in some service of the day – or at least once a week.

The Kyries are not necessarily penitential. They can be used as responses to intercessions as at the Midday Office. But they can be used as an alternative way of expressing sorrow for our sins. *Kyrie Eleison*, 'Lord, have mercy', has been used in the church from the earliest times. It is the only piece of worship that has survived in its Greek form into present-day worship. It is thought to come from the words of the tax-collector in Luke 18.13. It is also seen as a summary of the 'Jesus Prayer' – 'Lord Jesus Christ, Son of God, have mercy on me, a sinner.' Expressing our desire for God's 'loving-kindness', it is a wider plea than for forgiveness.

The Intercessions that are written out are only for guidelines; it would be good to create your own. Or you could adapt them to your own needs, still using the printed responses. A good pattern for intercession is to remember in turn, the church, the world and its needs, the locality you live in, your own home and loved ones, the sick and needy, the departed.

The Collect is meant to be a summing up, a collecting together, of our prayers and thoughts that have gone before.

The final **Affirmation** declares God's relationship towards us with the desire that we carry an awareness of that relationship around with us.

It is good to follow this with the **Grace** or the **Blessing** said by all together if possible (see page 126).

THEMES FOR EACH DAY

Each day is devised to look at some of the eternal realities of our God. After celebrating the joy of the resurrection on Sunday we spend a day each with God the Father, Christ the Saviour, and the Holy Spirit the Life giver. Thursday is concerned with church and community, Friday is the day on which we remember the passion of our Lord. On Saturday we give thanks for the communion of saints and remember the coming of our Lord in glory. Obviously, if we want to, we can spend more time on any of these great events. It is a good practice to use one office until you know it well and then move on to another. So instead of using four offices a day for a week, you may like to use one a week for twenty-eight weeks, or you might like to use the offices as they relate to the seasons of the church. If you use only one a day, an occasional prayer may need a slight alteration in its wording.

Sunday is the day when Christ our Lord rose again. So we celebrate the resurrection. We celebrate the fact that death is conquered and that life is eternal. We rejoice in the presence of him who was dead but who is alive. We seek to experience the power of his resurrection and to know the risen Lord.

Monday, the first day of creation, is when we celebrate the fact that God made the world, God loves the world, God is within his world and the world in him. We seek to love the world with the great love that God has for the world and to act responsibly towards his creation.

On **Tuesday**, we give thanks that for us and for our salvation our Lord Jesus Christ has come to dwell among us. We give thanks for the incarnation, for our Lord's life and ministry. We give thanks that He can be met in our meeting with others. We rejoice that the Word made flesh dwells among us.

On **Wednesday**, we rejoice in the power of the Holy Spirit. We give thanks for the gifts of the Spirit – but above all for the gift of the Spirit, that our God gives himself to us. We rejoice in the Lord and giver of life and give thanks for the life and abilities he gives to us.

On **Thursday**, we express our belief that God cares for his world and is at work within it. We give thanks for the work of the church. We commend our world, our church, our community to our God, knowing that he is at work in them and through them.

Friday is the day of the crucifixion. We remember the death and passion of our Lord. We pray especially for all who are suffering. We give thanks for our salvation and pray for the redeeming of all creation.

On **Saturday**, we give thanks for the saints of God. We rejoice in the fact that we have a share in the communion of saints. We give praise for their inspiration and example and pray that we may follow in their steps. The Night Office reminds us of the coming of our Lord, that he comes to each of us each day, and that he will come again in glory.

In a separate section there are some additional prayers and other items which may also be included in any of the offices as appropriate.

Sources of the material used, including those items marked with an asterisk (*), are given at the end of this book. Prayers and responses which have no acknowledgement have been written by myself, though often inspired by ancient prayers. It is hoped that, following this example, you will be inspired to write your own.

Sunday
RESURRECTION

Sunday Morning – Resurrection

———

Jesus Christ is risen from the dead. Alleluia!

(*Silence*)

Rejoice, heavenly powers! Sing, choirs of angels!
    Alleluia!
Christ our King is risen. Alleluia!
Exult, all creation! Rejoice, O earth, in shining
    splendour! Alleluia!
Christ our King is risen. Alleluia!
Christ has conquered! Glory fills you!
Christ our King is risen. Alleluia!
Darkness vanishes forever! Christ dispels the
    darkness of our night! Alleluia!
Christ our King is risen. Alleluia!

PSALM 100

Christ is risen. Alleluia!

Be joyful in the Lord, all you lands;
serve the Lord with gladness
and come before his presence with a song.

Know this: The Lord himself is God;
he himself has made us and we are his;
we are his people and the sheep of his pasture.

Enter his gates with thanksgiving;
go into his courts with praise;
give thanks to him and call upon his name.

For the Lord is good; his mercy is everlasting;
and his faithfulness endures from age to age.

Christ is risen. Alleluia!

Jesus said . . . 'I am the resurrection and the life. Those who believe in me, even though they die, will live, and everyone who lives and believes in me will never die.'

THE SONG OF CHRIST'S GLORY

At the name of Jesus every knee should bow.

Christ Jesus was in the form of God:
but he did not cling to equality with God.
At the name of Jesus every knee should bow.

He emptied himself, taking the form of a servant:
and was born in the likeness of men.
At the name of Jesus every knee should bow.

Being found in human form he humbled himself:
and became obedient unto death, even death
    on a cross.
At the name of Jesus every knee should bow.

Therefore God has highly exalted him:
and bestowed on him a name above every name;
At the name of Jesus every knee should bow.

that at the name of Jesus every knee should bow:
in heaven and on earth and under the earth;
At the name of Jesus every knee should bow.

and every tongue confess that Jesus Christ is Lord:
to the glory of God the Father.
At the name of Jesus every knee should bow.

Glory be to the Father, and to the Son;
and to the Holy Spirit:
as it was in the beginning, is now;
and shall be for ever. Amen.

At the name of Jesus every knee should bow.

Lord, have mercy upon us.
Christ, have mercy upon us.
Lord, have mercy upon us.

Our Father ...

That we may rejoice in the resurrection,
Risen Christ, give us hope.
That we may know that you have conquered death,
Risen Christ, give us hope.
That we may know that you have triumphed
  over the grave,
Risen Christ, give us hope.
That those in doubt and despair may see
  your light,
Risen Christ, give us hope.
That those who are troubled in mind may know
  your peace,
Risen Christ, give us hope.
That those in pain and distress may know your
  presence,
Risen Christ, give us hope.
That those caring for the terminally ill may know
  your power,
Risen Christ, give us hope.
That those who mourn may discover the joy of
  life eternal,
Risen Christ, give us hope.

Almighty Father, who in your great mercy made
glad the disciples with the sight of the risen Lord:
give us such knowledge of his presence with us,
that we may be strengthened and sustained by
his risen life and serve you continually in righteousness and truth: through Jesus Christ our Lord.
Amen.*

The God of hope, who brought again from the dead that great Shepherd of the sheep, Jesus Christ, fill us with all joy and peace in believing.

Sunday Midday – Resurrection

Alleluia! Christ is risen.
He is risen indeed. Alleluia!

(*Silence*)

He has conquered death. **Alleluia!**
He has triumphed over the grave.
    Alleluia!
He has defeated hell. **Alleluia!**
He has risen again. **Alleluia!**
Christ is alive. **Alleluia!**

PSALM 23

The Lord is my shepherd; I will fear no evil.

The Lord is my shepherd;
I shall not be in want.

He makes me lie down in green pastures;
and leads me beside still waters.

He revives my soul
and guides me along right pathways for his
    name's sake.

Though I walk through the valley
    of the shadow of death, I shall fear no evil;
for you are with me; your rod and your staff,
    they comfort me.

You spread a table before me in the presence
    of those who trouble me;
You have anointed my head with oil, and my
    cup is running over.

Surely goodness and mercy shall follow me all
    the days of my life,
and I will dwell in the house of the Lord for ever.

The Lord is my shepherd; I will fear no evil.

ROMANS 6.3–6
Do you not know that all of us who have been baptized
into Christ Jesus were baptized into his death? Therefore we have been buried with him by baptism into
death, so that, just as Christ was raised from the dead
by the glory of the Father, so we too might walk in
newness of life.

GLORY AND HONOUR

Glory to God in the highest.

Glory and honour and power:
are yours by right, O Lord our God:

for you created all things:
and by your will they have their being.

Glory and honour and power:
are yours by right, O Lamb who was slain;

16

for by your blood you ransomed men for God:
from every race and language, from every people
and nation,

to make them a kingdom of priests:
to stand and serve before our God.

To him who sits on the throne, and to the Lamb:
be praise and honour, glory and might, for ever
and ever. **Amen.**

Glory to God in the highest.

Risen Lord, we pray that you will uphold all
who are down.
Lord, have mercy.
Upon the world's poor and the unemployed,
Lord, have mercy.
Upon the homeless and the refugee,
Lord, have mercy.
Upon the war torn and the oppressed,
Christ, have mercy.
Upon the depressed and the despairing,
Christ, have mercy.
Upon the sinful and the sorrowful,
Christ, have mercy.
Upon the sick and the suffering,
Lord, have mercy.
Upon the diseased and the disgraced,
Lord, have mercy.
Upon the lonely and the dying,
Lord, have mercy.

Our Father . . .

Lord of all life and power, who through the mighty
resurrection of your Son overcame the old order of sin
and death to make all things new in him: grant that
we, being dead to sin and alive to you in Jesus Christ,

may reign with him in glory; to whom with you and the Holy Spirit be praise and honour, glory and might, now and in all eternity. **Amen.***

May you find in Christ Jesus, risen from the dead, a sure ground for your faith, a firm support for your hope, the assurance of sins forgiven, and life that is eternal.

Sunday Evening – Resurrection

Worthy is the Lamb who was slain to receive power and riches, wisdom and strength, and honour and glory and blessing. Alleluia!

(*Silence*)

That we may know you as the risen Lord,
Hear us, risen Christ.
That in you the downtrodden may find hope,
Hear us, risen Christ.
That in you the darkened lives may find light,
Hear us, risen Christ.
That in you we may rejoice that life is eternal,
Hear us, risen Christ.

Bless the Lord, O my soul.

Bless the Lord, O my soul,
and all that is within me, bless his holy name.

Bless the Lord, O my soul,
and forget not all his benefits.

He forgives all your sins
and heals all your infirmities;

He redeems your life from the grave
and crowns you with mercy and loving-kindness;

He satisfies you with good things,
and your youth is renewed like an eagle's.

The Lord executes righteousness
and judgement for all who are oppressed.

He made his way known to Moses
and his works to the children of Israel.

The Lord is full of compassion and mercy,
slow to anger and of great kindness . . .

The Lord has set his throne in heaven,
and his kingship has dominion over all.

Bless the Lord, you angels of his,
you mighty ones who do his bidding,
and hearken to the voice of his word.

Bless the Lord, all you his hosts,
you ministers of his who do his will.

Bless the Lord, all you works of his,
in all places of his dominion;
bless the Lord, O my soul.

Bless the Lord, O my soul.

JOHN 20.19

When it was evening on that day, the first day of the week, and the doors of the house where the disciples had met were locked for fear of the Jews, Jesus came and stood among them and said, 'Peace be with you.' After he said this, he showed them his hands and his side. Then the disciples rejoiced when they saw the Lord.

BLESSED BE GOD
1 PETER 1.3–5

Blessed be God. Alleluia!

Blessed be the God and Father of our Lord
    Jesus Christ!
Blessed be God. Alleluia!

By his great mercy he has given us a new birth
    into a living hope, through the resurrection
    of Jesus Christ from the dead;
Blessed be God. Alleluia!

and into an inheritance that is imperishable,
    undefiled, and unfading, kept in heaven
    for you;
Blessed be God. Alleluia!

who are being protected by the power of God
    through faith, for a salvation ready to be
    revealed in the last time.
Blessed be God. Alleluia!

Lord, have mercy . . .

Our Father . . .

Abide with us, Lord, for it is toward the evening and the day is far spent: abide with us, and with your whole church. Abide with us in the evening of the day, in the evening of life, in the evening of the world. Abide with us in your grace and mercy, in your holy Word and Sacrament, in your comfort and your blessing. Abide with us in the night of distress and fear, in the night of doubt and temptation, in the night of bitter death, when these shall overtake us. Abide with us and all your faithful ones, O Lord, in time and in eternity.

The peace and the power of the presence of the risen Lord be upon you and remain with you always.

Sunday Night – Resurrection

Almighty God, from whose love neither life nor death can separate us: let the whole company of heaven praise you; let the whole church throughout the world praise you. Let us this night praise you.

(*Silence*)

By your death upon the cross
Raise us, good Lord.
By your burial in the grave
Raise us, good Lord.

21

By your descending into hell
Raise us, good Lord.
By your mighty resurrection
Raise us, good Lord.
By your conquering death
Raise us, good Lord.
By your risen appearances
Raise us, good Lord.
By your presence among us
Raise us, good Lord.

PSALM 113

Praise the name of the Lord. Alleluia!

Alleluia!
Give praise, you servants of the Lord;
praise the name of the Lord.

Let the name of the Lord be blessed;
from this time forth for evermore.

From the rising of the sun to its going down
let the name of the Lord be praised.

The Lord is high above all nations,
and his glory above the heavens.

Who is like the Lord our God, who sits enthroned
    on high,
but stoops to behold the heavens and the earth?

He takes up the weak out of the dust
and lifts up the poor from the ashes.

He sets them with the princes,
with the princes of his people.

He makes the woman of a childless house
to be a joyful mother of children.

Praise the name of the Lord. Alleluia!

1 PETER 1.3–5

Blessed be the God and Father of our Lord Jesus Christ! By his great mercy he has given us a new birth into a living hope through the resurrection of Jesus Christ from the dead, and into an inheritance that is imperishable, undefiled, and unfading, kept in heaven for you, who are being protected by the power of God through faith for a salvation ready to be revealed in the last time.

GREAT AND WONDERFUL

Great and wonderful is our God. Alleluia!

Great and wonderful are your deeds, Lord God
    the Almighty:
just and true are your ways, O king of the nations.

Who shall not revere and praise your name,
    O Lord?
for you alone are holy.

All nations shall come and worship in your
    presence:
for your just dealings have been revealed.

To him who sits upon the throne, and to
    the Lamb:

be praise and honour, glory and might, for ever
    and ever. **Amen**.

Great and wonderful is our God. Alleluia!

Lord, have mercy . . .

Our Father . . .

With all who are in darkness and weariness
Stand among us in your risen power.
With all who are in doubt and despair
Stand among us in your risen power.
With all who are in trouble and fearfulness
Stand among us in your risen power.
With all who are in sickness and weakness
Stand among us in your risen power.
With all who are frail and at the point of death
Stand among us in your risen power.

Risen Lord, light of all peoples, who on the third day rose again from the dead, come, stand among us: dispel the darkness of night with your celestial brightness, that we may walk before you as in the day, and as children of light; to the glory of your name, risen Lord, with the Father and the Holy Spirit one God for ever and ever. **Amen**.

Christ, risen in glory, scatter the darkness before us, that we may walk as children of light until we come to that light which is eternal.

monday
CREATION

Monday Morning – Creation

——

To God the Father, who created the world;
To God the Son, who redeemed the world;
To God the Holy Spirit, who sustains the world;
Be all praise and glory, now and for ever. **Amen**.

(*Silence*)

Awaken us to your glory.
Dispel the darkness of night.
Awaken us to your glory.
Destroy our heaviness of heart.
Awaken us to your glory.
Cure the blindness of our sight.
Awaken us to your glory.
Heal the deafness of our ears.
Awaken us to your glory.
Open the mouth that is dumb.
Awaken us to your glory.
Restore a gentleness of touch.
Awaken us to your glory.
Encourage in us a sense of adventure.
Awaken us to your glory.
Bring us an awareness of you.
Awaken us to your glory.

PSALM 8

How exalted is your name in all the world!

O Lord our governor,
how exalted is your name in all the world!

Out of the mouths of infants and children
your majesty is praised above the heavens.

You have set up a stronghold against your
    adversaries,
to quell the enemy and the avenger.

When I consider your heavens, the work of
    your fingers,
the moon and the stars you have set in their
    courses,

What are mortals, that you should be mindful
    of them?
mere human beings, that you should seek
    them out?

You have made them little lower than the angels;
you adorn them with glory and honour.

You give them mastery over the works of
    your hands,
and put all things under their feet,

All sheep and oxen,
even the wild beasts of the field,

The birds of the air, the fish of the sea,
and whatsoever walks in the paths of the sea.

O Lord our governor,
how exalted is your name in all the world!

How exalted is your name in all the world!

GENESIS 1.1, 26, 31
In the beginning, when God created the heavens and
the earth . . . God said, 'Let us make humankind in our
own image, according to our likeness; and let them
have dominion over the fish of the sea, and over the
birds of the air, and over the cattle, and over all the wild
animals of the earth, and over every creeping thing
that creeps upon the earth.' . . . God saw everything
that he had made, and indeed, it was very good.

A SONG OF CREATION

Bless the Lord, all created things:
sing his praise and exalt him for ever.

Bless the Lord, you heavens:
bless the Lord, you angels of the Lord:
bless the Lord, all you his hosts:
bless the Lord, you waters above the heavens:
sing his praise and exalt him for ever.

Bless the Lord, sun and moon:
bless the Lord, you stars of heaven:
bless the Lord, all rain and dew:
sing his praise and exalt him for ever.

Bless the Lord, all winds that blow:
bless the Lord, you fire and heat:
bless the Lord, scorching wind and bitter cold:
sing his praise and exalt him for ever.

Bless the Lord, dews and falling snows:
bless the Lord, you nights and days:
bless the Lord, light and darkness:
sing his praise and exalt him for ever.

Bless the Lord, frost and cold:
bless the Lord, you ice and snow:
bless the Lord, lightnings and clouds:
sing his praise and exalt him for ever.

O let the earth bless the Lord:
bless the Lord, you mountains and hills:
bless the Lord, all that grows in the ground:
sing his praise and exalt him for ever.

Bless the Lord, you springs:
bless the Lord, you seas and rivers:
bless the Lord, you whales and all that swim
in the waters:
sing his praise and exalt him for ever.

Bless the Lord, all birds of the air:
bless the Lord, you beasts and cattle:
bless the Lord, all people on the earth:
sing his praise and exalt him for ever.

O people of God, bless the Lord:
bless the Lord, you priests of the Lord:
bless the Lord, you servants of the Lord:
sing his praise and exalt him for ever.

Bless the Lord, all you of upright spirit:
bless the Lord, you that are holy and humble
    in heart:
bless the Father, the Son and the Holy Spirit:
sing his praise and exalt him for ever.

Lord, have mercy . . .

Our Father . . .

To all explorers and scientists,
Father of all, give guidance.
To all artists and musicians,
Father of all, give guidance.
To all writers and broadcasters,
Father of all, give guidance.
To all who influence our lives,
Father of all, give guidance.
To all who strive for peace,
Father of all, give guidance.

How wonderful, O Lord, are the works of your hands!
The heavens declare your glory,
the arch of the sky displays your handiwork.
In your love you have given us the power
to behold the beauty of your world in all its
    splendour.

The sun and the stars, the valleys and the hills,
the rivers and the lakes, all disclose your presence.
The roaring breakers of the sea tell of your
  awesome might;
the beasts of the field and the birds of the air
  proclaim your wondrous will.
In your goodness you have made us able to
  hear the music of the world.
The voices of loved ones reveal to us that you
  are in our midst.
A divine song sings through all creation.*

The holy and life-giving God,
teach you to reverence all his works,
to praise him in all you do,
to share in his work of creation,
and to live to his glory.

Monday Midday – Creation

Creator, Father of all,
you give us life,
you give us love,
you give us yourself.
Help us to give
our lives,
our love,
ourselves, to you.

(Silence)

Whatever befalls the earth befalls the children
    of the earth.
Every part of the earth is sacred.
The air is precious, for all of us share the same breath.
Every part of the earth is sacred.
This we know, the earth does not belong to us;
we belong to the earth.
Every part of the earth is sacred.
This we know, all things are connected;
like the blood that unites one family.
Every part of the earth is sacred.
Our God is the same God,
whose compassion is equal for all;
Every part of the earth is sacred.
We did not weave the web of life;
we are merely a strand in it.
Every part of the earth is sacred.
Whatever we do to the web
we do to ourselves.
**Every part of the earth is sacred
For all belongs to our Creator.***

PSALM 95.1–7

The Lord our God is a great God.

Come, let us sing to the Lord;
let us shout for joy to the rock of our salvation.

Let us come before his presence with thanksgiving
and raise a loud shout to him with psalms.

For the Lord is a great God,
and a great king above all gods.

In his hand are the depths of the earth,
and the heights of the hills are his also.

The sea is his, for he made it,
and his hands have moulded the dry land.

Come, let us bow down and bend the knee,
and kneel before the Lord our Maker.

For he is our God,
and we are the people of his pasture,
and the sheep of his hand.

The Lord our God is a great God.

1 CHRONICLES 29.11–13
Yours, O Lord, are the greatness, the power, the glory,
the victory, and the majesty; for all that is in the heavens
and on the earth is yours; yours is the kingdom, O Lord,
and you are exalted as head above all. Riches and honour come from you, and you rule over all. In your hand
are power and might; and it is in your hand to make
great and to give strength to all. And now, our God,
we give thanks to you and praise your glorious name.

Upon all who seek to care for our world,
Lord, have mercy.
Upon all who seek to conserve and preserve
    the earth's goodness,
Lord, have mercy.
Upon all who work as your co-creators,
Lord, have mercy.
Upon those who work in dark or dangerous places,
Christ, have mercy.
Upon those who suffer through pollution,
Christ, have mercy.
Upon those whose land has been spoiled by war,
Christ, have mercy.
Upon those who work on the land or the sea,
Lord, have mercy.

Upon all artists, writers and craftspeople,
Lord, have mercy.
Upon all who seek to make this world beautiful,
Lord, have mercy.

Our Father ...

Lord our God, you renew the face of the earth
and bring newness to our world:
Restore the waters,
Refresh the air,
Revive the land,
Breathe new life into all your creation,
and begin with us.

The Lord, the Creator of heaven and earth,
bless and guide you in all that you do,
confirm and strengthen you in all goodness,
and keep you in life which is eternal.

Monday Evening – Creation

Lord, you created the day and the night,
you created darkness and light.
We commend to you this day
all that has happened in it.
Protect us through the night
until the morning light.

(Silence)

O Lord, open our lips,
And our mouth shall declare your praise.
O Lord, open our eyes,
That we may behold your presence.
O Lord, open our ears,
That we may hear your call.
O Lord, open our hearts,
That we may respond to your love.
O Lord, open our lives,
That we may rejoice in your creation.

PSALM 147.1–10; 15–21

Great is our Lord, and mighty is his power.

Alleluia!
How good it is to sing praises to our God!
How pleasant it is to honour him with praise!

The Lord rebuilds Jerusalem;
he gathers the exiles of Israel.

He heals the broken-hearted
and binds up their wounds.

He counts the number of the stars
and calls them all by their names.

Great is our Lord, and mighty in power;
there is no limit to his wisdom.

The Lord lifts up the lowly,
but casts the wicked to the ground.

Sing to the Lord with thanksgiving;
make music to our God upon the harp.

He covers the heavens with clouds
and prepares rain for the earth;

He makes grass to grow upon the mountains
and green plants to serve us all.

He provides food for flocks and herds
and for the young ravens when they cry . . .

He has established peace on your borders;
he satisfies you with the finest wheat.

He sends out his command to the earth,
and his word runs very swiftly.

He gives snow like wool;
he scatters hoar frost like ashes.

He scatters his hail like bread crumbs;
who can stand against his cold?

He sends forth his word and melts them;
he blows with his wind and the waters flow.

He declares his word to Jacob,
his statutes and judgements to Israel.

He has not done so to any other nation;
to them he has not revealed his judgements.
Alleluia!

Great is our Lord, and mighty is his power.

JOHN 1.1–5
In the beginning was the Word, and the Word was with
God, and the Word was God. He was in the beginning
with God. All things came into being through him, and
without him not one thing came into being. What has
come into being in him was life, and the life was the
light of all people. The light shines in the darkness,
and the darkness did not overcome it.

BLESSED BE GOD FOR EVER
ISAIAH 43.15–21

Blessed be God for ever.

I am the Lord, your Holy One,
the Creator of Israel, your King.
Blessed be God for ever.

Thus says the Lord, who makes a way in the sea,
a path in the mighty waters . . .
Blessed be God for ever.

I am about to do a new thing;
now it springs forth, do you not perceive it?
Blessed be God for ever.

I will make a way in the wilderness
and rivers in the desert.
Blessed be God for ever.

The wild animals will honour me,
the jackals and the ostriches;
Blessed be God for ever.

for I give water in the wilderness
rivers in the desert, to give drink to my chosen people;
Blessed be God for ever.

the people whom I formed for myself
so that they might declare my praise.
Blessed be God for ever.

Lord, have mercy . . .

Our Father . . .
Upon all who are suffering from hunger,
Lord, come in hope.
Upon the world's refugees,
Lord, come in hope.
Upon all prisoners of tyranny and war,
Lord, come in hope.

Upon all who are exploited,
Lord, come in hope.
Upon the underprivileged,
Lord, come in hope.
Upon all who are without work,
Lord, come in hope.

Father of all creation, we thank you that you
    have given us a world rich in resources,
and made us stewards of your mysteries;
help us to act responsibly,
not wasting or destroying what we do not need,
not polluting the earth, or sea or sky,
that we may act with love towards all things,
and so reflect the great love that you have for
    the world.

Be with us, Lord God, creator of all,
to strengthen us on our journey,
to guide us in all our doings,
that we may share in the love and care for
    your world.

Monday Night – Creation

Lord, you created the world
by your love.
You redeemed the world
through your love.

You maintain the world
with your love.
Help us to give our love to you,
Father, Son and Holy Spirit.

(*Silence*)

I believe, O God of all gods, that you are
the Creator of all things.
I believe, O God of all gods, that you are
the Lord and giver of life.
I believe, O God of all gods, that you are
the sustainer of all peoples.
I believe, O God of all gods, that you are
the giver of breath and spirit.
I believe, O God of all gods, that you are
the giver of body and mind.
I believe, O God of all gods, that you are
here and with us now.

PSALM 148

Praised be God our creator.

Alleluia!
Praise the Lord from the heavens,
praise him in the heights.

Praise him, all you angels of his;
praise him, all his host.

Praise him, sun and moon;
praise him, all you shining stars.

Praise him, heaven of heavens,
and you waters above the heavens.

Let them praise the name of the Lord;
for he commanded and they were created.

He made them stand fast for ever and ever;
he gave them a law which shall not pass away.

Praise the Lord from the earth,
you sea-monsters and all deeps;

Fire and hail, snow and fog,
tempestuous wind, doing his will;

Mountains and all hills,
fruit trees and all cedars;

Wild beasts and all cattle,
creeping things and winged birds;

Kings of the earth and all peoples,
princes and all rulers of the world;

Young men and maidens,
old and young together,

let them praise the name of the Lord,
for his name only is exalted,
his splendour is over earth and heaven.

He has raised up strength for his people
and praise for his loyal servants,
the children of Israel, a people who are near him.
Alleluia!

Praised be God our creator.

ROMANS 8.19–21
The creation waits with eager longing for the revealing
of the children of God; for the creation was subjected
to futility, not of its own will but by the will of the one
who subjected it, in hope that the creation itself will
be set free from its bondage to decay and will obtain
the freedom of the glory of the children of God.

Blessed are you, the God of our forebears,
worthy to be praised and exalted for ever.

Blessed is your holy and glorious name,
worthy to be praised and exalted for ever.

Blessed are you, glorious in your holy temple,
worthy to be praised and exalted for ever.

Blessed are you who behold the depths,
worthy to be praised and exalted for ever.

Blessed are you, enthroned on the cherubim,
worthy to be praised and exalted for ever.

Blessed are you on the throne of your kingdom,
worthy to be praised and exalted for ever.

Blessed are you in the heights of heaven,
worthy to be praised and exalted for ever.*

Lord, have mercy . . .

Our Father . . .

For the beauty of the earth,
Father of all, we praise you.
For the mystery of creation,
Father of all, we praise you.
For the wonders of the universe,
Father of all, we praise you.
For the power within all things,
Father of all, we praise you.
For all who work the land,
Creator, hear us.
For all who care for our planet,
Creator, hear us.

For all involved in conservation,
Creator, hear us.
For all who improve our environment,
Creator, hear us.

Almighty God, Creator of all things, Maker of
    all people,
grant that we may find a unity in you,
that we may be joined together in a bond of peace,
that we may share, with justice, the rich resources
    of the world,
that no one may be in hunger, or oppressed,
that none of your creation may be spoiled or
    misused.
We ask this in the name of him who gave
    himself for the world,
Jesus Christ our Lord. **Amen.**

God, who made the world, protect you this night.
Christ, who redeemed the world, give you peace
    this night.
The Spirit, who sustains the world, be with you
    this night.

Tuesday

INCARNATION

Tuesday Morning – Incarnation

Blessed are you, Lord Jesus Christ,
King of the Universe,
Yet born of the Virgin Mary.

(Silence)

The Lord is here.
His Spirit is with us.
Holy God,
Holy and Mighty One,
Holy and Strong One,
Abide in us.
Holy God,
Holy and Incarnate One,
Holy and Indwelling One,
Abide in us.
Holy God,
Holy and Life-giving One,
Holy and Guiding One,
Abide in us.

PSALM 18.1–10; 17–20

He parted the heavens and came down.

I love you, O Lord my strength,
O Lord my stronghold, my crag and my haven.

My God, my rock in whom I put my trust,
my shield, the horn of my salvation and my refuge;
you are worthy of praise.

I will call upon the Lord,
and so shall I be saved from my enemies.

The breakers of death rolled over me,
and the torrents of oblivion made me afraid.

The cords of hell entangled me,
and the snares of death were set for me.

I called upon the Lord in my distress
and cried out to my God for help.

He heard my voice from his heavenly dwelling;
my cry of anguish came to his ears.

The earth reeled and rocked;
the roots of the mountains shook;
they reeled because of his anger.

Smoke rose from his nostrils
and a consuming fire out of his mouth;
hot burning coals blazed forth from him.

He parted the heavens and came down
with a storm cloud under his feet . . .

He reached down from on high and grasped me;
he drew me out of great waters.

He delivered me from my strong enemies
and from those who hated me;
for they were too mighty for me.

They confronted me in the day of my disaster;
but the Lord was my support.

He brought me out into an open place;
he rescued me because he delighted in me.

He parted the heavens and came down.

JOHN 1.10–14

He was in the world, and the world came into being through him; yet the world did not know him. He came to what was his own, and his own people did not accept him. But to all who received him, who believed in his name, he gave power to become children of God, who were born, not of blood or of the will of the flesh or of the will of man, but of God. And the Word became flesh and lived among us, and we have seen his glory, the glory as of a father's only son, full of grace and truth.

BENEDICTUS

The dawn from on high shall break upon us.

Blessed be the Lord the God of Israel:
for he has come to his people and set them free.

He has raised up for us a mighty saviour:
born of the house of his servant David.

Through his holy prophets he promised of old:
that he would save us from our enemies,
from the hands of all that hate us.

He promised to show mercy to our fathers:
and to remember his holy covenant.

This was the oath he swore to our father Abraham:
to set us free from the hands of our enemies,

free to worship him without fear:
holy and righteous in his sight all the days of our life.

You, my child, shall be called the prophet of
the Most High:
for you will go before the Lord to prepare his way,

to give his people knowledge of salvation:
by the forgiveness of all their sins.

In the tender compassion of our God:
the dawn from on high shall break upon us,

to shine on those who dwell in darkness and
    the shadow of death:
and to guide our feet into the way of peace.

The dawn from on high shall break upon us.

Lord, have mercy . . .

Our Father . . .

Christ, heralded by the angels,
open our eyes to your presence.
O Lord, hear us. **Graciously hear us.**

Christ, born of the blessed Virgin,
teach us obedience to your word.
O Lord, hear us. **Graciously hear us.**

Christ, born in a stable,
give hope to the homeless.
O Lord, hear us. **Graciously hear us.**

Christ, visited by the shepherds,
strengthen all who work on the land.
O Lord, hear us. **Graciously hear us.**

Christ, adored by the wise men,
guide all rulers and governments.
O Lord, hear us. **Graciously hear us.**

Christ, exiled in Egypt,
give comfort to all refugees.
O Lord, hear us. **Graciously hear us.**

Father, you have revealed your love
by the coming of our Lord Jesus Christ into our world.
Help us to welcome him with joy,
and to make room for him in our lives and homes,

that we may abide in him and he in us;
Through the same Christ our Lord, who lives
   and reigns
with you, O Father, and the Holy Spirit, world
   without end. **Amen.**

May you see Christ in others,
Be Christ to others,
That we may dwell in him, and he in us.

Tuesday Midday – Incarnation

Blessed are you, Lord Jesus Christ.
You came down and took upon you our humanity,
that you might raise us up to share in your divinity.

(*Silence*)

By the obedience of Mary,
Lord made flesh
Dwell among us.
By the understanding of Joseph,
Lord made flesh
Dwell among us.
By the song of the angels,
Lord made flesh
Dwell among us.

By your birth in a manger,
Lord made flesh
Dwell among us.
By the adoration of the shepherds,
Lord made flesh
Dwell among us.
By the worship of the wise men,
Lord made flesh
Dwell among us.

PSALM 121

My help comes from the Lord.

I lift up my eyes to the hills;
from where is my help to come?

My help comes from the Lord,
the maker of heaven and earth.

He will not let your foot be moved
and he who watches over you will not fall asleep.

Behold, he who keeps watch over Israel
shall neither slumber nor sleep;

The Lord himself watches over you;
the Lord is your shade at your right hand,

So that the sun shall not strike you by day,
nor the moon by night.

The Lord shall preserve you from all evil;
it is he who shall keep you safe.

The Lord shall watch over your going out and
    your coming in,
from this time forth for evermore.

My help comes from the Lord.

LUKE 1.78–9
By the tender mercy of our God, the dawn from on
high will break upon us, to give light to those who sit
in darkness and in the shadow of death, to guide our
feet into the way of peace.

That the coming of Christ may disperse all
    darkness,
Lord, have mercy.
That the birth of Christ may hallow all life,
Lord, have mercy.
That the love of Christ may be in every heart,
Lord, have mercy.
That the peace of Christ may fill the world,
Christ, have mercy.
That the descent of Christ may uplift all peoples,
Christ, have mercy.
That the humility of Christ may teach us
    gentleness,
Christ, have mercy.
That the presence of Christ may be within us,
Lord, have mercy.
That the power of Christ may be upon us,
Lord, have mercy.
That the Spirit of Christ may fill us,
Lord, have mercy.

Our Father . . .

Lord, open our hearts to your love,
and make your home within us.
As you took upon you our nature,
grant that we may be partakers of the Divine.
Grant that we may ever rejoice in your presence,
King of kings and Lord of lords.

The Father, who has shown his love for us, be
   with us.
The Son, who has come to be among us, be
   with us.
The Spirit, who fills the whole world, be with us.
The Holy Three be within and without us, now
   and evermore.

Tuesday Evening – Incarnation

Blessed are you, Christ, Light of the world;
you descend into our darkness,
to lift us into the realms of light.

(*Silence*)

Let us bless the living God:

He was born of the Virgin Mary,
Revealed in his glory,

Worshipped by angels,
Proclaimed among the nations,

Believed in throughout the world,
Exalted in the highest heavens.

Glory to God in the highest
and peace to his people on earth.*

Let your ways be known upon earth.

May God be merciful to us and bless us,
show us the light of his countenance and
     come to us.

Let your ways be known upon earth,
your saving health among all nations.

Let the peoples praise you, O God;
let all the peoples praise you.

Let the nations be glad and sing for joy,
for you judge the peoples with equity
and guide all the nations upon earth.

Let the peoples praise you, O God;
let all the peoples praise you.

The earth has brought forth her increase;
may God, our own God, give us his blessing.

May God give us his blessing;
and may all the ends of the earth stand in
     awe of him.

Let your ways be known upon earth.

1 JOHN 4.7–11.
Beloved, let us love one another, because love is from
God; everyone who loves is born of God and knows
God. Whoever does not love does not know God, for
God is love. God's love was revealed among us in this
way: God sent his only Son into the world so that we
might live through him. In this is love, not that we
loved God but that he loved us and sent his Son to be
the atoning sacrifice for our sins. Beloved, since God
loved us so much, we also ought to love one another.

He has visited and redeemed his people.

My soul proclaims the greatness of the Lord:
my spirit rejoices in God my saviour;

for he has looked with favour on his lowly
    servant:
from this day all generations will call me
    blessed;

the Almighty has done great things for me:
and holy is his name.

He has mercy on those who fear him:
in every generation.

He has shown the strength of his arm:
he has scattered the proud in their conceit.

He has cast down the mighty from their
    thrones:
and has lifted up the lowly.

He has filled the hungry with good things:
and the rich he has sent away empty.

He has come to the help of his servant
    Israel:
for he has remembered his promise
    of mercy,

the promise he made to our fathers:
to Abraham and his children for ever.

He has visited and redeemed his people.

Lord, have mercy ...

Our Father ...

Jesus, born a refugee,
Come among us.
Jesus, friend of the poor,
Come among us.
Jesus, lover of the outcast,
Come among us.
Christ, food for the hungry,
Come among us.
Christ, health of the sick,
Come among us.
Christ, saviour of the world,
Come among us.
Jesus, bringer of good news,
Come among us.
Jesus, hope of us all,
Come among us.

Lord Jesus Christ, Son of Mary,
born into a human family,
let us know you in our homes.
Bless our families and our friends,
our neighbours and all your people.
Grant that we may rejoice that you
　　are made flesh and dwell among us,
Jesus Christ our Lord. **Amen**.

The Wonderful Counsellor guide you,
The Mighty God protect you,
The Everlasting Father be with you,
The Prince of Peace inspire you,
And the blessing of God be upon you, now
　　and evermore.

Tuesday Night – Incarnation

Christ, as a light,
illumine and guide us.
Christ, as a shield,
overshadow and cover us.
Christ be under us. Christ be over us.
Christ be beside us, on left and on right.
Christ be before us.
Christ be behind us.
Christ be within us.
Christ be without us.
Christ, as a light,
illumine and guide us.*

(*Silence*)

Christ is come among us.
Give glory.
Christ has come down from heaven.
Give glory.
Christ is on the earth.
Give glory.
Christ gives light to the world.
Give glory.
Christ is with us always.
Give glory.

Give thanks to the Lord, for he is good,
for his mercy endures for ever.

Give thanks to the God of gods,
for his mercy endures for ever.

Give thanks to the Lord of lords,
for his mercy endures for ever;

Who only does great wonders,
for his mercy endures for ever;

Who by his wisdom made the heavens,
for his mercy endures for ever;

Who spread out the earth upon the waters,
for his mercy endures for ever;

Who created great lights,
for his mercy endures for ever;

The sun to rule the day,
for his mercy endures for ever;

The moon and the stars to govern
    the night,
for his mercy endures for ever . . .

Who remembered us in our low estate,
for his mercy endures for ever;

And delivered us from our enemies,
for his mercy endures for ever;

Who gives food to all creatures,
for his mercy endures for ever.

Give thanks to the God of heaven,
for his mercy endures for ever.

1 JOHN 4.13–15

By this we know that we abide in him and he in us, because he has given us of his Spirit. And we have seen and do testify that the Father has sent his Son as the Saviour of the world. God abides in those who confess that Jesus is the Son of God, and they abide in God.

NUNC DIMITTIS

My own eyes have seen your salvation.

Lord, now you let your servant go in peace:
your word has been fulfilled.

My own eyes have seen the salvation:
which you have prepared in the sight of every
    people;

a light to reveal you to the nations:
and the glory of your people Israel.

My own eyes have seen your salvation.

Lord, have mercy . . .

Our Father . . .

In the power of the presence
Lord, may we abide.
In the love of the Lord
Lord, may we abide.
In the strength of the Saviour
Lord, may we abide.
In the compassion of Christ
Lord, may we abide.
In the joy of Jesus
Lord, may we abide.

In the indwelling of our God
Lord, may we abide.
That we may dwell in him and he in us
Lord, may we abide.

Almighty God, who by the incarnation of our Lord
Jesus Christ, dispelled the darkness of the world and
gave light to all peoples, protect us as the darkness
descends, and keep us ever in your light, and continue
to enlighten our lives by your great glory. Through
Christ our Lord, who lives and reigns with you and
the Holy Spirit, one God, world without end. **Amen**.

The glory of the Lord shine upon you, and scatter the
darkness from before your path, that you may ever
walk in his light.

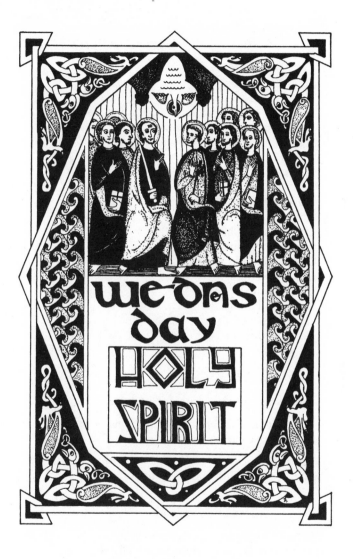

WEDNS
DAY
HOLY
SPIRIT

Wednesday Morning – Holy Spirit

The Spirit of the Lord fills the whole world.
The Spirit of the Lord moves over the deep.
The Spirit of the Lord warms our hearts.
The Spirit of the Lord fills all things.

(*Silence*)

Come, Holy Spirit, come,
Come and fill us.
Come, Lord of life, come,
Come and fill us.
Come, wind of heaven, come,
Come and fill us.
Come, flame of love, come,
Come and fill us.
Come, giver of all gifts, come,
Come and fill us.

PSALM 86.1–10

Keep watch over my life, for I am faithful.

Bow down your ear, O Lord, and answer me,
for I am poor and in misery.

Keep watch over my life, for I am faithful;
save your servant who trusts in you.

Be merciful to me, O Lord, for you are my God;
I call upon you all the day long.

Gladden the soul of your servant,
for to you, O Lord, I lift up my soul.

For you, O Lord, are good and forgiving,
and great is your love towards all who call upon you.

Give ear, O Lord, to my prayer,
and attend to the voice of my supplications.

In the time of my trouble I will call upon you,
for you will answer me.

Among the gods there is none like you, O Lord,
nor anything like your works.

All the nations you have made
will come and worship you, O Lord,
and glorify your name.

For you are great; you do wondrous things;
and you alone are God.

Keep watch over my life, for I am faithful.

JOEL 2.28–9
I will pour out my spirit on all flesh; your sons and your
daughters shall prophesy, your old men shall dream
dreams, and your young men shall see visions. Even
on the male and female slaves, in those days, I will
pour out my spirit.

A NEW SPIRIT
EZEKIEL 36.24–8

I will put a new Spirit within you.

I will take you from the nations,
and gather you from all the countries,
and bring you into your own land.

I will sprinkle clean water upon you,
and you shall be clean from all your uncleannesses,
and from all your idols I will cleanse you.

A new heart I will give you,
and a new spirit I will put within you;

and I will remove from your body the heart of stone
and give you a heart of flesh.

I will put my spirit within you,
and make you follow my statutes
and be careful to observe my ordinances.

Then you shall live in the land that I gave to
    your ancestors;
and you shall be my people, and I will be your God.

I will put a new Spirit within you.

Lord, have mercy . . .

Our Father . . .

Spirit of God, you give life to the world.
Breathe on us, breath of God.
Spirit of God, you give guidance to all rulers.
Breathe on us, breath of God.
Spirit of God, you give talents to all peoples.
Breathe on us, breath of God.
Spirit of God, you direct all artists and craftspeople.
Breathe on us, breath of God.
Spirit of God, you give comfort to the troubled.
Breathe on us, breath of God.
Spirit of God, you renew your church.
Breathe on us, breath of God.

The strength of God guide us.
The power of God preserve us.
The wisdom of God instruct us.
The Spirit of God be within us,
This day and evermore;
This day and evermore.

Go out in the power of the Spirit, to live and
    work to his glory.

Wednesday Midday – Holy Spirit

Send out your Holy Spirit, O Lord,
and renew the face of the earth.

(*Silence*)

Come, Holy Spirit.
Come among us,
Come, Holy Spirit.
Come as the wind to move us,
Come, Holy Spirit.
Come as the fire to prove us,
Come, Holy Spirit.
Come, Power of all powers,
Renew us.
Come, Holy Spirit.
Come, Strength of all strengths,
Refresh us.
Come, Holy Spirit.
Come, Might of all mighty ones,
Revive us.
Come, Holy Spirit.

Let your good Spirit lead me.

Lord hear my prayer,
and in your faithfulness heed my supplications;
answer me in your righteousness.

Enter not into judgement with your servant,
for in your sight shall no one living be justified.

For my enemy has sought my life
and has crushed me to the ground;
making me live in dark places
like those who are long dead.

My spirit faints within me;
my heart within me is desolate.

I remember the time past:
I muse upon all your deeds;
I consider the works of your hands.

I spread out my hands to you;
my soul gasps to you like a thirsty land:

O Lord, make haste to answer me; my spirit
    fails me;
do not hide your face from me
or I shall be like those who go down to the Pit.

Let me hear of your loving-kindness in the
    morning,
for I put my trust in you;
show me the road that I must walk,
for I lift my soul to you.

Deliver me from my enemies, O Lord,
for I flee to you for refuge.

Teach me to do what pleases you, for you are my God;
let your good Spirit lead me on level ground

Revive me, O Lord, for your name's sake;
for your righteousness' sake, bring me out of trouble.

Let your good Spirit lead me.

ACTS 2.1–4
When the day of Pentecost had come, they were all
together in one place. And suddenly from heaven
there came a sound like the rush of a violent wind,
and it filled the entire house where they were sitting.
Divided tongues, as of fire, appeared among them,
and a tongue rested on each of them. All of them were
filled with the Holy Spirit and began to speak in other
languages, as the Spirit gave them ability.

YOU ARE IN THE SPIRIT
ROMANS 8.9–11

His Spirit dwells in us.

You are in the Spirit,
since the Spirit of God dwells in you.

Anyone who does not have the Spirit of Christ
does not belong to him.

But if Christ is in you,
though the body is dead because of sin,
the spirit is life because of righteousness.

If the Spirit of him who raised Jesus from the
    dead dwells in you,
he who raised Christ from the dead will give
    life to your mortal bodies also
through his Spirit that dwells in you.

His Spirit dwells in us.

On all who are dis-spirited and dejected,
Lord, have mercy.
On all who have lost hope or joy,
Lord, have mercy.
On all who are unable to cope,
Lord, have mercy.
On all who are weak and heavy-burdened,
Christ, have mercy.
On all who are fearful and anxious,
Christ, have mercy.
On all who are lost or have strayed,
Christ, have mercy.
On all who feel lifeless and dead,
Lord, have mercy.
On all who feel forsaken and betrayed,
Lord, have mercy.
On all who are powerless and helpless,
Lord, have mercy.

Our Father ...

Lord, you have taught us that all our doings without
love are nothing worth. Send your Holy Spirit and
pour into our hearts that most excellent gift of love,
the true bond of peace and all virtues, without which,
whosoever lives is counted dead before you. Grant this
for the sake of your only Son, Jesus Christ our Lord.*

God the Father, bless us;
Christ the Son, take care of us;
Holy Spirit, enlighten us
all the days of our life.

Wednesday Evening – Holy Spirit

———

All who are led by the Spirit of God are children of God. By this we know that we abide in him and he in us, because he has given us of his Spirit.*

(*Silence*)

They were all filled with the Holy Ghost.
Fill us, Holy Spirit.
When the doors are closed and we are afraid
    to move,
Fill us, Holy Spirit.
When we are weak and unable to act,
Fill us, Holy Spirit.
When we are hesitant and unable to speak,
Fill us, Holy Spirit.
When we lack energy and are unable to cope,
Fill us, Holy Spirit.
That we may go out in your power,
Fill us, Holy Spirit.
That we may live and work for you,
Fill us, Holy Spirit.
That we may be part of your mission,
Fill us, Holy Spirit.

The Spirit of God is in all the world.

Lord, you have searched me out and
    known me;
you know my sitting down and my rising up;
you discern my thoughts from afar.

You trace my journeys and my resting-places
and are acquainted with all my ways.

Indeed, there is not a word on my lips,
but you, O Lord, know it altogether.

You press upon me behind and before
and lay your hand upon me.

Such knowledge is too wonderful for me;
it is so high that I cannot attain to it.

Where can I go then from your Spirit?
where can I flee from your presence?

If I climb up to heaven, you are there;
if I make the grave my bed, you are
    there also.

If I take the wings of the morning
and dwell in the uttermost parts of the sea,

Even there your hand will lead me
and your right hand hold me fast.

If I say, 'Surely the darkness will cover me,
and the light around me turn to night',

Darkness is not dark to you;
the night is as bright as the day;
darkness and light to you are both alike.

For you yourself created my inmost parts;
you knit me together in my mother's womb.

I will thank you because I am marvellously made;
your works are wonderful and I know it well.

The Spirit of God is in all the world.

ROMANS 5.5
God's love has been poured into our hearts through
the Holy Spirit that has been given to us.

Lord, have mercy ...

Our Father ...

Holy Spirit, bringing order out of chaos,
Come, renew the face of the earth.
Holy Spirit, breathing life into the lifeless,
Come, renew the face of the earth.
Holy Spirit, making strong the weak,
Come, renew the face of the earth.
Holy Spirit, giving talents to your people,
Come, renew the face of the earth.
Holy Spirit, guiding all who venture,
Come, renew the face of the earth.
Holy Spirit, filling all things,
Come, renew the face of the earth.

Almighty God, without you we are not able to
    please you.
Mercifully grant that your Holy Spirit may in all
    things direct and rule our hearts; through
    Jesus Christ our Lord.*

The God of hope fill you with all joy and peace
    in believing,
that you may abound in hope through the power
    of the Holy Spirit.

Wednesday Night – Holy Spirit

————

The Spirit of the Lord fills the whole world.
    Alleluia! Alleluia!
In him all things have their being. Alleluia!
    Alleluia!

(*Silence*)

Come, Holy Spirit,
Restore the lives which without you are dead.
Come, Holy Spirit.
Kindle the hearts which without you are dull
    and cold.
Come, Holy Spirit.
Enlighten the minds which without you are
    dark and blind.
Come, Holy Spirit.
Fill the church which without you is an empty shrine,
Come, Holy Spirit.
and teach us how to pray.
Come, Holy Spirit.*

PSALM 29

God shall give strength to his people.

Ascribe to the Lord, you gods,
ascribe to the Lord glory and strength.

Ascribe to the Lord the glory due to his name;
worship the Lord in the beauty of holiness.

The voice of the Lord is upon the waters;
the God of glory thunders;
the Lord is upon the mighty waters.

The voice of the Lord is a powerful voice;
the voice of the Lord is a voice of splendour.

The voice of the Lord breaks the cedar trees;
the Lord breaks the cedars of Lebanon:

He makes Lebanon skip like a calf;
and Mount Hermon like a young wild ox.

The voice of the Lord splits the flames of fire;
the voice of the Lord shakes the wilderness;
the Lord shakes the wilderness of Kadesh.

The voice of the Lord makes the oak trees writhe
and strips the forest bare.

And in the temple of the Lord
all are crying, 'Glory!'

The Lord sits enthroned above the flood;
the Lord sits enthroned as king for evermore.

The Lord shall give strength to his people;
the Lord shall give his people the blessing
    of peace.

God shall give strength to his people.

ROMANS 15.13
May the God of hope fill you with all joy and peace
in believing, so that you may abound in hope by the
power of the Holy Spirit.

THE SONG OF THE SPIRIT
ISAIAH 61.1–3

The Spirit of the Lord God is upon me.

The spirit of the Lord God is upon me,
because the Lord has anointed me;

he has sent me to bring good news to the
    oppressed,
to bind up the broken-hearted,

to proclaim liberty to the captives,
and release to the prisoners;

to proclaim the year of the Lord's favour,
and the day of vengeance of our God;
to comfort all who mourn;

to provide for those who mourn in Zion –
to give them a garland instead of ashes,

the oil of gladness instead of mourning,
the mantle of praise instead of a faint spirit.

The Spirit of the Lord God is upon me.

Lord, have mercy . . .

Our Father . . .

We pray for the newly baptized;
Hear us, O Holy Spirit.
For the recently confirmed,
Hear us, O Holy Spirit.
For all testing their vocations,
Hear us, O Holy Spirit.
For all bishops, priests and deacons,
Hear us, O Holy Spirit.
For all ministers of word and sacrament,
Hear us, O Holy Spirit.
For all who seek to witness to your power,
Hear us, O Holy Spirit.
For the powerless, and all who are troubled
    this night,
Hear us, O Holy Spirit.

Almighty and everlasting God, by whose Spirit the
whole body of the Church is governed and sanctified:
hear our prayer which we offer for all your faithful
people; that each in their vocation and ministry may
serve you in holiness and truth to the glory of your
name; through our Lord and Saviour Jesus Christ.*

The Spirit of truth lead you into all truth,
and give you grace to confess that Jesus
    Christ is Lord,
and to proclaim the word and works of God.

73

Thursday
COMMUNITY

Thursday Morning – Community

Blessed be the Lord God of heaven and earth, for he has visited and redeemed his people. He has raised up a mighty salvation for us in Christ Jesus our Lord.

(*Silence*)

The Father is with us.
Amen.
The Creator is with you,
And also with you.
Jesus is with us.
Amen.
The Saviour is with you,
And also with you.
The Spirit is with us.
Amen.
The Strengthener is with you,
And also with you.
God is with us.
Amen.

PSALM 84

Happy are the people who trust in you.

How dear to me is your dwelling, O Lord
   of hosts!
My soul has a desire and longing
for the courts of the Lord;
my heart and my flesh rejoice in the living God.

The sparrow has found her a house
and the swallow a nest where she may lay her young;
by the side of your altars, O Lord of hosts,
my King and my God.

Happy are the people who dwell in your house!
they will always be praising you.

Happy are the people whose strength is in you!
whose hearts are set on the pilgrims' way.

Those who go through the desolate valley
will find it a place of springs;
for the early rains have covered it with pools
    of water.

They will climb from height to height,
and the God of gods will reveal himself in Zion.

Lord God of hosts, hear my prayer;
hearken, O God of Jacob.

Behold our defender, O God;
and look upon the face of your anointed.

For one day in your courts
is better than a thousand in my own room,
and to stand at the threshold of the house of
    my God
than to dwell in the tents of the wicked.

For the Lord God is both sun and shield;
he will give grace and glory;

No good thing will the Lord withhold
from those who walk with integrity.

O Lord of hosts,
happy are they who put their trust in you!

Happy are the people who trust in you.

DEUTERONOMY 6.4–5
The Lord is our God, the Lord alone. You shall love
the Lord your God with all your heart, and with all
your soul, and with all your might.

EVERLASTING PEACE
ISAIAH 2.3–4

That he may teach us his ways

'Come, let us go up to the mountain of the Lord,
to the house of the God of Jacob;

that he may teach us his ways
and that we may walk in his paths.'

For out of Zion shall go forth instruction,
and the word of the Lord from Jerusalem.

He shall judge between the nations,
and shall arbitrate for many peoples;

they shall beat their swords into ploughshares,
and their spears into pruning-hooks;

nation shall not lift up sword against nation,
neither shall they learn war any more.

That he may teach us his ways.

Lord, have mercy . . .

Our Father . . .

That the church may show its unity in Christ,
Lord, hear us.
Lord, graciously hear us.
That all churches may work together for the
      benefit of all peoples,
Lord, hear us.
Lord, graciously hear us.

That all movements towards unity may prosper,
Lord, hear us.
Lord, graciously hear us.
That divisions and conflicts may cease,
Lord, hear us.
Lord, graciously hear us.
That the world may find a lasting peace,
Lord, hear us.
Lord, graciously hear us.
That none may hunger or thirst,
Lord, hear us.
Lord, graciously hear us.

Almighty God, give us wisdom to perceive you,
intelligence to understand you,
diligence to seek you,
patience to wait for you,
vision to behold you,
a heart to meditate upon you,
a life to proclaim you;
through Jesus Christ our Lord,
who lives with you and the Holy Spirit,
one God now and for ever.*

Lord, be with us to guide us,
within us to strengthen us,
without us to protect us,
above us to raise us,
beneath us to uphold us,
before us to lead us,
behind us to guard us,
ever about us,
this day and evermore;
this day and evermore.

Thursday Midday – Community

You, O Lord, are in the midst of us and we are
    called by your name;
leave us not, O Lord our God.

(Silence)

Glory be to you, O God.
Glory be to you.
Glory be to you, O Father.
Glory be to you.
Glory be to you, O Son.
Glory be to you.
Glory be to you, O Spirit.
Glory be to you.
Glory be to you, O God.
Glory be to you.

PSALM 145.1–9

Your faithful servants bless you.

I will exalt you, O God my King,
and bless your name for ever and ever.

Every day will I bless you
and praise your name for ever and ever.

Great is the Lord and greatly to be praised;
there is no end to his greatness.

One generation shall praise your works to
another
and shall declare your power.

I will ponder the glorious splendour of your
majesty
and all your marvellous works.

They shall speak of the might of your
wondrous acts,
and I will tell of your greatness.

They shall publish the remembrance of your
great goodness;
they shall sing of your righteous deeds.

The Lord is gracious and full of compassion,
slow to anger and of great kindness.

The Lord is loving to everyone
and his compassion is over all his works.

Your faithful servants bless you.

EPHESIANS 3.16–19
I pray that, according to the riches of his glory, he may
grant that you may be strengthened in your inner being with power through his Spirit, and that Christ may
dwell in your hearts through faith, as you are being
rooted and grounded in love. I pray that you may have
the power to comprehend, with all the saints, what is
the breadth and length and height and depth, and to
know the love of Christ that surpasses knowledge; so
that you may be filled with all the fullness of God.

THE BREAD OF HEAVEN
WISDOM 16.20–1

You gave your people food of angels,
and without their toil you supplied them from heaven
with bread ready to eat,
Lord, give us this bread.

providing every pleasure
and suited to every taste.
Lord, give us this bread.

For your sustenance manifested your sweetness
towards your children;
Lord, give us this bread.

and the bread, ministering to the desire of the
   one who took it,
was changed to suit everyone's liking.
Lord, give us this bread.

That the barriers that divide us may be broken down,
Lord, have mercy.
That we may live in unity, peace and concord,
Lord, have mercy.
That we may come to mutual understanding
   and care,
Lord, have mercy.
Upon all who suffer from dissensions and quarrels,
Christ, have mercy.
Upon all who are torn apart by war and by violence,
Christ, have mercy.
Upon all who are divided in their loyalty and love,
Christ, have mercy.
That all who work for unity may be blessed,
Lord, have mercy.
That all who heal divisions may have hope,
Lord, have mercy.
That all who lead nations may seek peace,
Lord, have mercy.

Our Father . . .

God be in my head, and in my understanding.
God be in my eyes, and in my looking.
God be in my mouth, and in my speaking.
God be in my heart, and in my thinking.
God be at my end, and at my departing.*

The Lord enrich us with his grace, and further
    us with his heavenly blessing:
the Lord defend us in adversity, and keep us
    from all evil;
the Lord receive our prayers, and graciously
    absolve us from our offences.*

Thursday Evening – Community

Blessed are you, Creator of all things;
the heavens adore you.
Let the whole earth worship you.
Let all peoples proclaim you.
Let all nations obey you.
Let us serve you in love and in peace.

(Silence)

Come, Lord, and rule.
Come into our hearts
and fill them with love.
Come, Lord, and rule.
Come into our minds
and fill them with peace.
Come, Lord, and rule.
Come into our lives
and fill them with light.
Come, Lord, and rule.
Come into our days
and fill them with glory.
Come, Lord, and rule.

PSALM 138

Great is the glory of the Lord.

I will give thanks to you, O Lord, with my
    whole heart;
before the gods I will sing your praise.

I will bow down towards your holy temple
and praise your name,
because of your love and faithfulness.

For you have glorified your name
and your word above all things.

When I called, you answered me;
you increased my strength within me.

All the kings of the earth will praise you, O Lord,
when they have heard the words of your mouth.

They will sing of the ways of the Lord,
that great is the glory of the Lord.

Though the Lord be high, he cares for the lowly;
he perceives the haughty from afar.

Though I walk in the midst of trouble, you keep
    me safe;
you stretch forth your hand against the fury of
    my enemies;
your right hand shall save me.

The Lord will make good his purpose for me;
O Lord, your love endures for ever;
do not abandon the work of your hands.

Great is the glory of the Lord.

EPHESIANS 4.1–6
I therefore, the prisoner in the Lord, beg you to lead
a life worthy of the calling to which you have been
called, with all humility and gentleness, with patience,
bearing with one another in love, making every effort
to maintain the unity of the Spirit in the bond of peace.
There is one body and one Spirit, just as you were
called to the one hope of your calling, one Lord, one
faith, one baptism, one God and Father of all, who is
above all and through all and in all.

GOD'S LOVE
1 JOHN 4.7–12

Let us love one another.

Beloved, let us love one another,
because love is from God;
Let us love one another.

Everyone who loves is born of God and knows God.
Whoever does not love does not know God,
    for God is love..
Let us love one another.

God's love was revealed among us in this way:
God sent his only Son into the world so that
we might live through him.
Let us love one another.

In this is love, not that we loved God but that
he loved us
and sent his Son to be the atoning sacrifice for
our sins.
Let us love one another.

Beloved, since God loved us so much,
we also ought to love one another.
Let us love one another.

No one has ever seen God;
if we love one another God lives in us,
and his love is perfected in us.
Let us love one another.

Lord, have mercy . . .

Our Father . . .

For the whole church that it may be one,
Hear us, good Lord.
For all who work for peace, unity and concord,
Hear us, good Lord.
For the work of the United Nations and
peace-keeping forces,
Hear us, good Lord.
For those who maintain the law and
administer justice,
Hear us, good Lord.
For all who influence our future,
Hear us, good Lord.
For all in government and positions of authority,
Hear us, good Lord.

O Lord, support us all the day long of this troublous
life, until the shades lengthen and the evening comes,
and the busy world is hushed, the fever of life is over,
and our work is done. Then Lord, in your mercy, grant
us safe lodging, a holy rest and peace at the last;
through Jesus Christ our Lord, who lives and reigns
with you, one God for ever. **Amen.***

God the Father, who created you,
God the Son, who redeemed you,
God the Spirit, who sanctifies you,
Bless and keep you, now and evermore.

Thursday Night – Community

Lord, let your love fill our hearts and minds, that we
may love the world with the great love that you have
for the world; that we may love you with all our heart
and mind and soul and strength, and our neighbour
as ourselves.

(Silence)

O Lord, open our eyes
To behold your presence.
O Lord, open our ears
To hear your voice.

O Lord, open our hearts
To receive your love.
O Lord open our lips,
And our mouth shall proclaim your praise.
Glory be to the Father, and to the Son, and to
the Holy Spirit:
**As it was in the beginning, is now, and shall be
for ever. Amen.**

PSALM 111

I will give thanks to the Lord with my whole heart.

Alleluia!
I will give thanks to the Lord with my whole heart,
in the assembly of the upright, in the congregation.

Great are the deeds of the Lord!
they are studied by all who delight in them.

His work is full of majesty and splendour,
and his righteousness endures for ever.

He makes his marvellous works to be remembered;
the Lord is gracious and full of compassion.

He gives food to those who fear him;
he is ever mindful of his covenant.

He has shown his people the power of his works
in giving them the lands of the nations.

The works of his hands are faithfulness and justice;
all his commandments are sure.

They stand fast for ever and ever,
because they are done in truth and equity.

He sent redemption to his people;
he commanded his covenant for ever;
holy and awesome is his name.

The fear of the Lord is the beginning of wisdom;
those who act accordingly have a good
    understanding;
his praise endures for ever.

I will give thanks to the Lord with my whole heart.

1 PETER 2.9–10
You are a chosen race, a royal priesthood, a holy
nation, God's own people, in order that you may
proclaim the mighty acts of him who called you out of
darkness into his marvellous light. Once you were not
a people, but now you are God's people; once you had
not received mercy, but now you have received mercy.

ARISE AND SHINE
ISAIAH 60.1–3

Arise, shine; for your light has come,
and the glory of the Lord has risen upon you.
The Lord has risen upon us.

For darkness shall cover the earth,
and thick darkness the peoples;
The Lord has risen upon us.

but the Lord will arise upon you,
and his glory will appear over you.
The Lord has risen upon us.

Nations shall come to your light,
and kings to the brightness of your dawn.
The Lord has risen upon us.

Lord, have mercy . . .

Our Father . . .

Upon the one, holy, catholic and apostolic church,
Come, Spirit of God.
Upon your faithful people in their witness,
Come, Spirit of God.
Upon all who proclaim the gospel,
Come, Spirit of God.
Upon all who declare your presence and love,
Come, Spirit of God.
Upon all who administer the sacraments,
Come, Spirit of God.
Upon those who are new in the faith,
Come, Spirit of God.
Upon all who are in doubt or despair,
Come, Spirit of God.

Gracious Father, we humbly beseech you for your
holy catholic church.
Fill it with all truth;
and all truth with all peace.
Where it is corrupt, purge it;
where it is in error, direct it;
where it is superstitious, rectify it;
where anything is amiss, reform it;
where it is right, strengthen and confirm it;
where it is in want, furnish it;
where it is divided and rent asunder,
make up the breaches of it,
O Holy One of Israel;
for the sake of Jesus Christ our Lord and Saviour.
Amen.*

Preserve us, O Lord, waking, and guard us while
sleeping,
that awake we may watch with Christ,
and asleep we may rest in peace.*

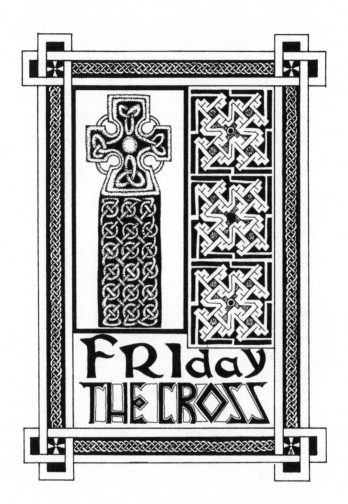

FRIday
THECROSS

Friday Morning – The Cross

We adore you, O Christ, and we bless you,
Because by your holy cross you have redeemed
the world.

(*Silence*)

Jesus, Lamb of God,
have mercy on us.
Jesus, bearer of our sins,
have mercy on us.
Jesus, redeemer of the world,
give us your peace.*

PSALM 31.1–5

Lord, make haste to deliver me.

In you, O Lord, have I taken refuge;
let me never be put to shame,
deliver me in your righteousness.

Incline your ear to me;
make haste to deliver me.

Be my strong rock, a castle to keep me safe,
for you are my crag and my stronghold;
for the sake of your name, lead me and guide me.

Take me out of the net that they have secretly
set for me,
for you are my tower of strength.

Into your hands I commend my spirit;
for you have redeemed me,
O Lord, O God of truth.

Lord, make haste to deliver me.

JOHN 3.16–17
For God so loved the world that he gave his only Son,
so that everyone who believes in him may not perish
but may have eternal life. Indeed, God did not send
the Son into the world to condemn the world, but in
order that the world might be saved through him.

SALVATOR MUNDI
We look to you to save and help us.

Jesus, saviour of the world, come to us in
    your mercy;
we look to you to save and help us.
We look to you to save and help us.

By your cross and your life laid down, you set
    your people free:
we look to you to save and help us.
We look to you to save and help us.

When they were ready to perish, you saved
    your disciples:
we look to you to come to our help.
We look to you to save and help us.

In the greatness of your mercy, loose us from
    our chains:
forgive the sins of all your people.
We look to you to save and help us.

Make yourself known as our Saviour and Mighty
    Deliverer:
save and help us, that we may praise you.
We look to you to save and help us.

Come now, and dwell with us, Lord Christ Jesus:
hear our prayer and be with us always.
We look to you to save and help us.

And when you come in your glory,
make us to be one with you
and to share the life of your kingdom.

We look to you to save and help us.*

Lord, have mercy . . .

Our Father . . .

To your cross, O Lord, we come for healing,
For you alone can make us whole.
We come with the broken-hearted and
    broken-spirited,
For you alone can make us whole.
We come with those with broken relationships,
For you alone can make us whole.
We come with the broken in body or in mind,
For you alone can make us whole.
We come with the weak and the handicapped,
For you alone can make us whole.
We come with the sinners and the guilty,
For you alone can make us whole.

Thanks be to you, my Lord Jesus Christ,
for all the benefits which you have won for me,
for all the pains and insults you have borne for me.
O most merciful Redeemer, Friend and Brother,
may I know you more clearly,
love you more dearly,
and follow you more nearly,
day by day.*

Christ, who was crucified, and now is risen, may we
find in you a sure ground for our faith, a firm support
for our hopes, the knowledge of sins forgiven, and
the assurance that life is eternal.

Friday Midday – The Cross

O Saviour of the world, who by your cross and
    precious blood have redeemed us,
Save us and help us we humbly beseech
    you, O Lord.

(Silence)

By your holy incarnation,
Good Lord, deliver us.
By your coming down among us,
Good Lord, deliver us.

By your being scorned and rejected,
Good Lord, deliver us.
By your cross and passion,
Good Lord, deliver us.
By your holy death and burial,
Good Lord, deliver us.
By your descending into hell,
Good Lord, deliver us.
By your mighty resurrection,
Good Lord, deliver us.

PSALM 51.1–13

Have mercy on me, O God.

Have mercy on me, O God,
according to your loving-kindness;
in your great compassion blot out my offences.

Wash me through and through from my wickedness
and cleanse me from my sin.

For I know my transgressions,
and my sin is ever before me.

Against you only have I sinned,
and done what is evil in your sight.

And so you are justified when you speak
and upright in your judgement.

Indeed, I have been wicked from my birth,
a sinner from my mother's womb.

For behold, you look for truth deep within me;
and will make me understand wisdom secretly.

Purge me from my sin and I shall be pure;
wash me and I shall be clean indeed.

Make me hear of joy and gladness,
that the body you have broken may rejoice.

Hide your face from my sins
and blot out all my iniquities.

Create in me a clean heart, O God,
and renew a right spirit within me.

Cast me not away from your presence
and take not your Holy Spirit from me.

Give me the joy of your saving help again
and sustain me with your bountiful Spirit.

Have mercy on me, O God.

ROMANS 5.6–8
For while we were still weak, at the right time Christ
died for the ungodly. Indeed, rarely will anyone die
for a righteous person – though perhaps for a good
person someone might actually dare to die. But God
proves his love for us in that while we were still sinners
Christ died for us.

THE SUFFERING SERVANT
ISAIAH 53.2–5

By his wounds we are healed.

He had no form or majesty that we should
    look at him,
nothing in his appearance that we should
    desire him.

He was despised and rejected by others;
a man of suffering and acquainted with infirmity;

and as one from whom others hide their faces
he was despised, and we held him of no account.

Surely he has borne our infirmities and carried
    our diseases;
yet we accounted him stricken, struck down
    by God, and afflicted.

But he was wounded for our transgressions,
crushed for our iniquities;

upon him was the punishment that made us whole,
and by his bruises we are healed.

By his wounds we are healed.

Christ who died for our sins, forgive the penitent.
Lord, have mercy.
Christ who shared our griefs, comfort the sorrowing.
Lord, have mercy.
Christ who thirsted on the cross, bring relief to
    the hungry.
Lord, have mercy.
Christ forsaken by all, be with the lonely and
    the sad.
Christ, have mercy.
Christ mocked and scorned, support the outcasts
    and rejected.
Christ, have mercy.
Christ who suffered great pain, be a strength
    to the weak.
Christ, have mercy.
Christ who died for us all, grant us your salvation.
Lord, have mercy.
Christ crucified, done to death and buried, give
    us hope.
Lord, have mercy.
Christ who descended into hell, raise us to glory.
Lord have mercy.

Our Father . . .

Teach us, good Lord, to serve thee as thou
     deservest;
to give and not to count the cost;
to fight and not to heed the wounds;
to toil and not to seek for rest;
to labour and not to ask for any reward,
save that of knowing that we do thy will.*

Christ, who by his death destroyed death,
raise you up to the life which is eternal.

Friday Evening – The Cross

Worthy is the Lamb who was slain, to receive power
and wealth and wisdom and might and honour and
glory and blessing!*

(*Silence*)

Lord, by your cross and passion, free us from evil
and deliver us.
Destroy the powers of darkness
and deliver us.
Free your creation from corruption
and deliver us.
Bring us to the liberty of the children of God
and deliver us.

My God, in whom I put my trust.

He who dwells in the shelter of the Most High,
abides under the shadow of the Almighty.

He shall say to the Lord:
'You are my refuge and my stronghold,
my God in whom I put my trust.'

He shall deliver you from the snare of the hunter
and from the deadly pestilence.

He shall cover you with his pinions,
and you shall find refuge under his wings;
his faithfulness shall be a shield and buckler.

You shall not be afraid of any terror by night,
nor of the arrow that flies by day;

Of the plague that stalks in the darkness,
nor of the sickness that lays waste at midday.

A thousand shall fall at your side
and ten thousand at your right hand,
but it shall not come near you.

Your eyes have only to behold
to see the reward of the wicked.

Because you have made the Lord your refuge,
and the Most High your habitation,

There shall no evil happen to you,
neither shall any plague come near your dwelling.

For he shall give his angels charge over you,
to keep you in all your ways.

They shall bear you in their hands,
lest you dash your foot against a stone.

You shall tread upon the lion and adder;
you shall trample the young lion and the serpent
    under your feet.

Because he is bound to me in love,
therefore will I deliver him;
I will protect him, because he knows my name.

He shall call upon me and I will answer him;
I am with him in trouble,
I will rescue him and bring him to honour.

With long life will I satisfy him,
and show him my salvation.

My God, in whom I put my trust.

2 CORINTHIANS 5.14–15
The love of Christ urges us on, because we are
convinced that one has died for all; therefore all have
died. And he died for all, so that those who live might
live no longer for themselves, but for him who died
and was raised for them.

BLESSED BE GOD FOREVER
EPHESIANS 1.3–7

Blessed be God forever.

Blessed be the God and Father of our Lord
    Jesus Christ,
who has blessed us in Christ with every spiritual
    blessing
in the heavenly places;
Blessed be God forever.

just as he chose us in Christ before the foundation
    of the world
to be holy and blameless before him in love.
Blessed be God forever.

He destined us for adoption as his children
through Jesus Christ, according to the good
    pleasure of his will,
Blessed be God forever.

to the praise of his glorious grace
that he freely bestowed on us in the Beloved.
Blessed be God forever.

In him we have redemption through his blood,
the forgiveness of our trespasses,
according to the richness of his grace
that he lavished on us.
Blessed be God forever.

Lord, have mercy . . .

Our Father . . .

By the nails through your hands and feet,
Give comfort to the suffering.
Hear us, Lord Christ.
By the crown of thorns upon your head,
Give hope to the despairing.
Hear us, Lord Christ.
By the spear that pierced your side,
Give courage to the heart-broken.
Hear us, Lord Christ.
By your being scorned and rejected of men,
Give love to the lonely.
Hear us, Lord Christ.
By your time of desolation,
Lift up all who are down.
Hear us, Lord Christ.
By your death on the cross,
Give us life which is eternal.
Hear us, Lord Christ.

O Lord and Master, Jesus Christ,
Word of the everlasting Father,
you have borne our grief
and carried the burden of our human frailty;
by the power of the Holy Spirit,
renew in your church gifts of healing,
and send out your disciples again
to preach the gospel of your kingdom,
to heal the sick,
and to relieve the sufferings of your children
to the praise and glory of your holy name. **Amen***.

By your passion protect us.
By your wounds heal us.
By your death raise us up.
And bring us to life eternal.

Friday Night – The Cross

To him who loves us, and freed us from our
    sins by his blood,
and made us to be a kingdom, priests serving
    his God and Father,
to him be glory and dominion for ever and
    ever. **Amen**.

(Silence)

Upon all who have been forsaken,
Lord, come in your mercy.
Upon all who have been betrayed by a kiss,
Lord, come in your mercy.
Upon all who are deserted by friends,
Lord, come in your mercy.
Upon all misunderstood by loved ones,
Lord, come in your mercy.
Upon all who are in physical pain,
Lord, come in your mercy.
Upon all suffering mental anguish,
Lord, come in your mercy.
Upon all at the point of death,
Lord, come in your mercy.

PSALM 142

O Lord, you are my refuge.

I cry to the Lord with my voice;
to the Lord I make loud supplication.

I pour out my complaint before him
and tell him all my trouble.

When my spirit languishes within me, you know
my path;
in the way wherein I walk they have hidden a
trap for me.

I look to my right hand and find no one who
knows me;
I have no place to flee to and no one cares for me.

I cry out to you, O Lord;
I say, 'You are my refuge, my portion in the
land of the living.'

Listen to my cry for help, for I have been brought
very low;

save me from those who pursue me, for they are
too strong for me.

Bring me out of prison, that I may give thanks
to your name;
when you have dealt bountifully with me, the
righteous will gather around me.

O Lord, you are my refuge.

1 PETER 2.24–5
He himself bore our sins in his body on the cross, so
that, free from sins, we might live for righteousness;
by his wounds you have been healed. For you were
going astray like sheep, but now you have returned
to the shepherd and guardian of your souls.

THE END OF DEATH
REVELATION 21.3–4
Death will be no more.

See, the home of God is among mortals.
He will dwell with them;
Death will be no more.

they will be his peoples
and God himself will be with them;
Death will be no more.

he will wipe every tear from their eyes.
Death will be no more;
Death will be no more.

mourning and crying and pain will be no more,
for the first things have passed away.
Death will be no more.

Lord, have mercy . . .

Our Father . . .

With broken hopes and broken promises,
we come to you, Lord,
for you alone can make us whole.
With broken relationships and broken hearts,
we come to you, Lord,
for you alone can make us whole.
With the broken in body and the broken in mind,
we come to you, Lord,
for you alone can make us whole.
With the broken in spirit and the despairing,
we come to you, Lord,
for you alone can make us whole.

Lord Jesus Christ,
Son of the living God,
who at this evening hour rested in the sepulchre,
and sanctified the grave
to be a bed of hope to your people:
make us so deeply sorry for our sins,
which were the cause of your passion,
that when our bodies lie in the dust,
our souls may live with you;
for with the Father and the Holy Spirit
you live and reign, now and forever. **Amen.***

Through his wounds may you find healing;
through his pain may you find relief;
Through his suffering may you find freedom;
Through his cross may you find victory.

Saturday

THE SAINTS

Saturday Morning – The Saints

———

Blessed are you, Lord God, revealed in your saints.
Through your holy ones you give us a glimpse
   of your glory.

(*Silence*)

Holy and Strong One, Holy and Mighty One,
Extend our vision.
and make us to be numbered with your saints.
Increase our faith
and make us to be numbered with your saints.
Direct our thoughts
and make us to be numbered with your saints.
Be in our words
and make us to be numbered with your saints.
Inspire our actions
and make us to be numbered with your saints.

PSALM 24

Bring us with your saints to glory.

The earth is the Lord's and all that is in it,
the world and all who dwell therein.

For it is he who founded it upon the seas
and made it firm upon the rivers of the deep.

'Who can ascend the hill of the Lord?
and who can stand in his holy place?'

'Those who have clean hands and a pure heart,
who have not pledged themselves to falsehood,
nor sworn by what is a fraud.

'They shall receive a blessing from the Lord
and a just reward from the God of their
    salvation.'

Such is the generation of those who
    seek him,
of those who seek your face, O God
    of Jacob.

Lift up your heads, O gates;
lift them high, O everlasting doors;
and the King of glory shall come in.

'Who is this King of glory?'
'The Lord strong and mighty,
the Lord mighty in battle.'

Lift up your heads, O gates;
lift them high, O everlasting doors;
and the King of glory shall come in.

'Who is he, this King of glory?'
'The Lord of hosts,
he is the King of glory.'

Bring us with your saints to glory.

HEBREWS 12.1–2
Therefore, since we are surrounded by so great a
cloud of witnesses, let us also lay aside every weight
and the sin that clings so closely, and let us run with
perseverance the race that is set before us, looking to
Jesus the pioneer and perfecter of our faith, who for
the sake of the joy that was set before him endured
the cross, disregarding its shame, and has taken his
seat at the right hand of the throne of God.

TE DEUM LAUDAMUS

You are God, and we praise you:
you are the Lord, and we acclaim you;

you are the eternal Father:
all creation worships you.

To you all angels, all the powers of heaven:
cherubim and seraphim, sing in endless praise,

Holy, holy, holy Lord, God of power and might:
heaven and earth are full of your glory.

The glorious company of apostles praise you:
the noble fellowship of prophets praise you;
the white-robed army of martyrs praise you.

Throughout the world the holy church acclaims you:
Father of majesty unbounded;

your true and only Son, worthy of all worship:
and the Holy Spirit, advocate and guide.

You, Christ, are the King of glory:
the eternal Son of the Father.

When you became man to set us free:
you did not abhor the Virgin's womb.

You overcame the sting of death:
and opened the kingdom of heaven to all believers.

You are seated at God's right hand in glory:
we believe that you will come and be our judge.

Come then, Lord, and help your people:
bought with the price of your own blood;

and bring us with your saints:
to glory everlasting.

Lord, have mercy . . .

Our Father . . .

For calling us to be your people,
We praise you, O God.
For giving us a share in the inheritance of
    your saints,
We praise you, O God.
For all who have taught us the faith,
We praise you, O God.
For all who have inspired us,
We praise you, O God.
For all who have guided us and been an example,
We praise you, O God.
That we may do what you would have us do,
Good Lord, hear us.
That we may be the people you would have us be,
Good Lord, hear us.

O Lord, grant that in following the example of your
saints, we may live holy and godly lives, and inspired
by their witness may steadfastly dedicate ourselves to
serve you and live to your glory, through Jesus Christ
our Lord, who lives and reigns with you and the Holy
Spirit, one God world without end.

Lord, fill our lives with
the alleluias of angels,
the hosannas of heaven,
and the sanctity of the saints.

Saturday Midday – The Saints

———

With angels and archangels, and with all the company
of heaven, we proclaim your great and glorious name,
for ever praising you and saying: Holy, holy, holy Lord,
God of power and might, heaven and earth are full of
your glory. Hosanna in the highest.*

(Silence)

With the saints, we believe and trust
in God the Father who made all things.
We believe and trust in him.
With the saints, we believe and trust
in His Son Jesus Christ who redeemed the world.
We believe and trust in him.
With the saints, we believe and trust
in the Holy Spirit who gives life to the people of God.
We believe and trust in him.
This is the faith of the saints of God.
This is our faith.
We believe and trust in one God,
Father, Son and Holy Spirit. Amen.

PSALM 1

Lord, here am I to do your will.

Happy are they who have not walked in the
    counsel of the wicked,
nor lingered in the way of sinners,
nor sat in the seats of the scornful!

Their delight is in the law of the Lord,
and they meditate on his law day and night.

They are like trees planted by streams of water,
bearing fruit in due season,
with leaves that do not wither;
everything they do shall prosper.

It is not so with the wicked:
they are like chaff which the wind blows away;

Therefore the wicked shall not stand upright
    when judgement comes,
nor the sinner in the council of the righteous.

For the Lord knows the way of the righteous,
but the way of the wicked is doomed.

Lord, here am I to do your will.

REVELATION 7.9–10
There was a great multitude that no one could count,
from every nation, from all tribes and peoples and
languages, standing before the throne and before the
Lamb, robed in white, with palm branches in their
hands. They cried out in a loud voice, saying, 'Salvation
belongs to our God who is seated on the throne, and
to the Lamb!'

THE CITY OF GOD
HEBREWS 12.22–4

Lord, open our eyes to your glory.

You have come to Mount Zion
and to the city of the living God,
the heavenly Jerusalem,
Lord, open our eyes to your glory.

and to innumerable angels
in festal gathering,
Lord, open our eyes to your glory.

and to the assembly of the firstborn
who are enrolled in heaven,
Lord, open our eyes to your glory.

and to God the judge of all,
and to the spirits of the righteous made perfect,
Lord, open our eyes to your glory.

and to Jesus,
the mediator of a new covenant.
Lord, open our eyes to your glory.

Our Father . . .

Upon your church, that it may be faithful to the
     gospel,
Lord, have mercy.
Upon your people, that they may show your love,
Lord, have mercy.
Upon your chosen ones, that they may do
     your will,
Lord, have mercy.
Upon all who are seeking to answer your call,
Christ, have mercy.
Upon all who are trying to proclaim your word,
Christ, have mercy.
Upon all who are seeking to serve you,
Christ, have mercy.
Upon all whose talents are being extended,
Lord, have mercy.
Upon all whose vocations are being tested,
Lord, have mercy.
Upon all whose lives are being tried,
Lord, have mercy.

Almighty God, you have knit together your elect into one communion and fellowship in the mystical body of your Son. Give us grace to follow your blessed saints in all virtuous and godly living, that we may come to those unspeakable joys which you have prepared for those who truly love you: through Jesus Christ our Lord.*

God give you grace to follow his saints
in love and joy and peace.

Saturday Evening – All Saints

Come, bless the Lord, all you servants of the Lord, who stand by night in the house of the Lord!*

(*Silence*)

God, the Father of heaven,
With your saints we worship you.
Christ, the hope of all the world,
With your saints we worship you.
Holy Spirit, who sanctifies the people of God,
With your saints we worship you.

PSALM 146

The Lord loves the righteous.

Alleluia!
Praise the Lord, O my soul!
I will praise the Lord as long as I live;
I will sing praises to my God while I have my being.

Put not your trust in rulers,
nor in any child of earth,
for there is no help in them.

When they breathe their last, they return to earth,
and in that day their thoughts perish.

Happy are they who have the God of Jacob for
    their help!
whose hope is in the Lord their God;

Who made heaven and earth, the seas, and all
    that is in them;
who keeps his promise for ever;

Who gives justice to those who are oppressed,
and food to those who hunger.

The Lord sets the prisoners free;
the Lord opens the eyes of the blind;
the Lord lifts up those who are bowed down;

The Lord loves the righteous;
the Lord cares for the stranger;
he sustains the orphan and widow,
but frustrates the way of the wicked.

The Lord shall reign for ever,
your God, O Zion, throughout all generations.
Alleluia!

The Lord loves the righteous.

EPHESIANS 4.11–13
The gifts he gave were that some would be apostles, some prophets, some evangelists, some pastors and teachers, to equip the saints for the work of ministry, for building up the body of Christ, until all of us come to the unity of faith and of the knowledge of the Son of God, to maturity, to the measure of the full stature of Christ.

THE BEATITUDES
MATTHEW 5.3–10

Blessed are the poor in spirit,
for theirs is the kingdom of heaven.
Theirs is the kingdom of heaven.

Blessed are those who mourn,
for they will be comforted.
Theirs is the kingdom of heaven.

Blessed are the meek,
for they will inherit the earth.
Theirs is the kingdom of heaven.

Blessed are those who hunger and thirst for
righteousness,
for they will be filled.
Theirs is the kingdom of heaven.

Blessed are the merciful,
for they will receive mercy.
Theirs is the kingdom of heaven.

Blessed are the pure in heart,
for they will see God.
Theirs is the kingdom of heaven.

Blessed are the peacemakers,
for they will be called children of God.
Theirs is the kingdom of heaven.

Blessed are those who are persecuted for
    righteousness' sake,
for theirs is the kingdom of heaven.
Theirs is the kingdom of heaven.

Lord, have mercy . . .

Our Father . . .

That we may remember always those who have
    gone before us,
God of the saints, **hear us**.
That we may be inspired by the noble works of old,
God of the saints, **hear us**.
That we may seek to follow the example of
    the saints,
God of the saints, **hear us**.
That the church may stand for truth and justice,
God of the saints, **hear us**.
That we may be unafraid to proclaim the gospel,
God of the saints, **hear us**.
That we may lead others to worship you,
God of the saints, **hear us**.
That we may bring your light to dark places,
God of the saints, **hear us**.

Watch, dear Lord, with those who wake, or watch, or
weep tonight, and give your angels charge over those
who sleep. Tend your sick ones, O Lord Christ; rest
your weary ones; bless your dying ones; soothe your
suffering ones; pity your afflicted ones; shield your
joyous ones. And all for your love's sake.*

The power and peace of the Presence protect you.
The grace and goodness of the saints inspire you.
The good and gracious God go with you and
    keep you always.

Saturday Night – Advent,
The Coming One

In the presence, in the peace, in the power of
God. **Amen**.

The Lord is here.
His Spirit is with us.

(*Silence*)

Come, Lord, awaken us to your presence.
Dispel the darkness of night.
Come, Lord, awaken us to your presence.
Cure the deafness of our ears.
Come, Lord, awaken us to your presence.
Heal the blindness of our sight.
Come, Lord, awaken us to your presence.
Open the mouths that are dumb.
Come, Lord, awaken us to your presence.
Stir a warmth in our hearts.
Come, Lord, awaken us to your presence.
Make us aware of you.
Come, Lord, awaken us to your presence.

PSALM 130

My soul is waiting for you, O Lord.

Out of the depths have I called to you, O Lord;
Lord, hear my voice;
let your ears consider well the voice of my
    supplication.
My soul is waiting for you, O Lord.

If you, Lord, were to note what is done amiss,
O Lord, who could stand?
My soul is waiting for you, O Lord.

For there is forgiveness with you;
therefore you shall be feared.
My soul is waiting for you, O Lord.

I wait for the Lord; my soul waits for him;
in his word is my hope.
My soul is waiting for you, O Lord.

My soul waits for the Lord,
more than the night-watch for the morning,
more than the night-watch for the morning.
My soul is waiting for you, O Lord.

O Israel, wait for the Lord,
for with the Lord there is mercy;
My soul is waiting for you, O Lord.

With him there is plenteous redemption,
and he shall redeem Israel from all their sins.
My soul is waiting for you, O Lord.

MARK 13.35–7
Keep awake – for you do not know when the master
of the house will come, in the evening, or at midnight,
or at cockcrow, or at dawn, or else he may find you
asleep when he comes suddenly. And what I say to
you I say to all: Keep awake.

(Silence)

Lord, when you appear, find us working,
 watching and waiting for you.
Amen. So come, Lord Jesus.

ADVENT CANTICLE

Eternal God, who through the coming of the
 Lord has revealed yourself as our Father,
Come.
Eternal Son, who became man for us and our
 salvation,
Come.
Eternal Spirit, who overshadowed the
 blessed Virgin,
Come.
Come, Lord, come down, come in, come
 among us.
Come.
Into our lack of vision,
Come.
Into our hardness of heart,
Come.
Into our loss of joy,
Come.

Lord have mercy . . .

Our Father . . .

Into our world of darkness,
Into our places of strife,
Into our troubles and weakness,
Come, Lord.
Come down, come in, come among us.

Into our joys and celebrations,
Into our homes and to our loved ones,
Into our work and our achievements,
Come, Lord.
Come down, come in, come among us.

To those who are in need,
To those who are in sickness,
To those who are in despair,
Come, Lord.
Come down, come in, come among us.

Christ is the Morning Star who, when the darkness of
this world is past, brings to his saints the promise of
the light of life and opens everlasting day.*

Almighty God, give us grace to cast away the works
of darkness and to put on the armour of light, now in
the time of this mortal life, in which your Son Jesus
Christ came to us in great humility, so that on the last
day, when he shall come again in his glorious majesty
to judge the living and the dead, we may rise to the life
immortal, through him who is alive and reigns with
you and the Holy Spirit, One God, now and for ever.
Amen.*

Good and gracious God, come;
come and abide with us,
come and guide us,
come and protect us,
this day and evermore. **Amen.**

Additional Prayers

——

These prayers can be added to any service and should be used at least once a week if not every day.

The **Gloria** may be said after each psalm and canticle:

Glory be to the Father, and to the Son, and to
the Holy Spirit:
**As it was in the beginning, is now, and shall
be for ever, world without end. Amen.**

The **Kyries** can be threefold, sixfold or ninefold, in English or in Greek. They are not necessarily penitential, and can be used as responses to our prayers for others, as is done at the midday services.

In the threefold Kyries, the leader says: 'Lord, have mercy (upon us)', and the others present reply: '**Christ, have mercy (upon us)**'. The leader then repeats: 'Lord, have mercy (upon us)'.

For the sixfold Kyries the group repeats each phrase after the leader. I like to think of the Kyries as directed to Father, Son and Holy Spirit in turn, though all can be directed to the Christ.

Below is printed the ninefold version, in English and in Greek:

Lord, have mercy (upon us).	Kyrie Eleison.
Lord, have mercy (upon us).	**Kyrie Eleison**.
Lord, have mercy (upon us).	Kyrie Eleison.
Christ, have mercy (upon us).	**Christe Eleison**.
Christ, have mercy (upon us).	Christe Eleison.
Christ, have mercy (upon us).	**Christe Eleison**.
Lord, have mercy (upon us).	Kyrie Eleison.
Lord, have mercy (upon us).	**Kyrie Eleison**.
Lord, have mercy (upon us).	Kyrie Eleison.

If the Kyries are used as a confession and plea for forgiveness, at their close these words can be added:

Almighty God, have mercy upon us, pardon and deliver us from all our sins, and keep us in life eternal, through Jesus Christ our Lord. **Amen**.

Once in the day the **Confession** may be said:

Let us confess our sins, in penitence and faith, firmly resolved to keep God's commandments and to live in love and peace with everyone.

Almighty God, our heavenly Father,
we have sinned against you and against our
  neighbours,
in thought and word and deed,
through negligence, through weakness,
through our own deliberate fault.
We are truly sorry and repent of all our sins.
For the sake of your Son Jesus Christ, who
  died for us,
forgive us all that is past;
and grant that we may serve you in newness of life
to the glory of your name. Amen.

Almighty God,
who forgives all who truly repent,
have mercy upon us,
pardon and deliver us from all our sins,
confirm and strengthen us in all goodness,
and keep us in life eternal;
through Jesus Christ our Lord. **Amen**.

GLORIA IN EXCELSIS
Glory to God in the highest,
and peace to his people on earth.
Lord God, heavenly King,
almighty God and Father,
we worship you, we give you thanks,
we praise you for your glory.
Lord Jesus Christ, only Son of the Father,
Lord God, Lamb of God,
you take away the sin of the world:
have mercy on us;
you are seated at the right hand of the Father:
receive our prayer.
For you alone are the Holy One,
you alone are the Lord,
you alone are the Most High,
Jesus Christ,
with the Holy Spirit,
in the glory of the Father. Amen.

THE APOSTLES' CREED
I believe in God, the Father almighty,
creator of heaven and earth.
I believe in Jesus Christ, his only Son, our Lord.
He was conceived by the power of the Holy Spirit
and born of the Virgin Mary.
He suffered under Pontius Pilate,
was crucified, died, and was buried.
He descended to the dead.
On the third day he rose again.
He ascended into heaven,
and is seated at the right hand of the Father.
He will come again to judge the living and
    the dead.
I believe in the Holy Spirit,
the holy catholic church,
the communion of saints,

the forgiveness of sins,
the resurrection of the body,
and the life everlasting. Amen.

At the end of each office may be said the **Grace**
or a **Blessing**:

**The grace of our Lord Jesus Christ, and the love of
God, and the fellowship of the Holy Spirit, be with us
all evermore.**

or

The blessing of God almighty, the Father, the Son,
and the Holy Spirit, be among us, and remain with us
always. **Amen.**

Acknowledgements and Sources

The Psalms are taken from the *Standard Book of Common Prayer* of the Episcopal Church of the USA, with the adaptations as in *Celebrating Common Prayer* (Mowbrays 1992). They are used with the permission of the Secretary for Liturgy of the Society of Saint Francis.

Scripture readings, and canticles based on identified scripture passages are, unless otherwise indicated, taken from the *New Standard Revised Version of the Bible*, Anglicized Edition (Oxford University Press 1995), copyright © 1995 by the Division of Christian Education of the National Council of the Churches of Christ in the United States of America, and are used by permission. All rights reserved.

Other canticles are, unless otherwise attributed, from the *Alternative Service Book 1980* of the Church of England, copyright © 1980 The Central Board of Finance of the Church of England, and are used by permission.

The prayers and responses which have no acknowledgement are of my own composition.

Sources of readings, prayers and canticles marked with an asterisk in the text are as follows:

SUNDAY
Almighty Father, who . . . *Alternative Service Book (ASB)*, Collect for the 1st Sunday after Easter
Lord of all life . . . *ASB*, Collect for Easter Day
Abide with us Lord . . . from Lutheran Church

MONDAY
How wonderful, O Lord . . . Jewish prayer
Whatever befalls the earth . . . Adapted from a speech by Chief Seattle, 1854
The Song of the Three *Celebrating Common Prayer*, p. 210

TUESDAY

Let us bless . . . *The Promise of His Glory* (Church House Publishing 1990), p. 153

Christ, as a light . . . Adapted from an ancient Celtic prayer

WEDNESDAY

Lord, you have taught us . . . *ASB*, Collect for the 7th Sunday after Pentecost

All who are led . . . Romans 8.14; 1 John 4.13 *NRSV*

Almighty God, without you . . . *ASB*, Collect for the 6th Sunday after Pentecost

Come, Holy Spirit . . . Source unknown

Almighty and everlasting God . . . *ASB*, Collect for the 2nd Sunday after Pentecost

THURSDAY

Almighty God, give us . . . Saint Benedict

God be in my head . . . *Sarum Primer*

The Lord enrich us . . . *Gregorian Sacramentary*

O Lord, support us . . . Cardinal John Henry Newman

Gracious Father . . . Archbishop William Laud

Preserve us, O Lord . . . Prayer from 'Night Prayer' in *Lent, Holy Week and Easter* (Church House Publishing/Cambridge University Press/SPCK 1986)

FRIDAY

Jesus, Lamb of God . . . *ASB* Eucharist

Salvator Mundi Based on a prayer of Henry Allon

Thanks be to you . . . St Richard of Chichester

Teach us, good Lord . . . St Ignatius Loyola

Worthy is the Lamb . . . Revelation 5.12 *Revised Standard Version*

O Lord and Master . . . Liturgy of Saint Mark, 5th century

Lord, Jesus Christ . . . Prayer from 'Night Prayer' in *Lent, Holy Week and Easter*

SATURDAY

With angels and archangels . . . *ASB* Eucharistic prayer

Almighty God, you have knit . . . *ASB*, Collect for All
Saints Day

Come, bless the Lord . . . Psalm 134.1 *NRSV*

Watch, dear Lord . . . St Augustine

Christ is the morning star . . . The Venerable Bede

Almighty God, give us grace . . . *ASB*, Collect for
Advent Sunday

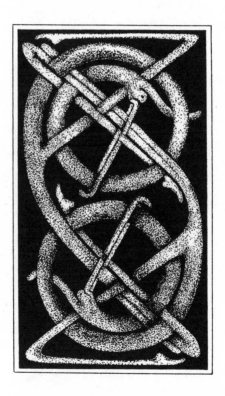

Other books by David Adam,
published by Morehouse:

THE EDGE OF GLORY
Prayers in the Celtic Tradition

Modern prayers which recapture the Celtic way of
intertwining divine glory with the ordinariness
of everyday events.

THE CRY OF THE DEER
Meditations on the Hymn of St. Patrick

Meditations leading to practical exercises which take us
deeper into the prayer experience in affirming the
Presence of God.

THE OPEN GATE
Celtic Prayers for Growing Spiritually

Readers pass through gates of spiritual discovery to
worlds filled with the mystery and glory of God. Prayers
of confession, adoration, intercession, and thanksgiving
provide structure for devotional life.